barcode 2pgp.in

barcode 2pgp.in

f
DT
512
L56
1999

*Conflict,
Conciliation, and
Civil Society in
Northern Ghana*

Building
Sustainable
Peace

Ada van der Linde
and Rachel Naylor

oxfam working **papers**

Building Sustainable Peace:
Conflict, Conciliation, and Civil Society
in Northern Ghana

Ada van der Linde and Rachel Naylor

An Oxfam Working Paper

First published by Oxfam GB in 1999

© Oxfam GB 1999

ISBN 0 85598 423 6

A catalogue record for this publication is available from the British Library.

Available from the following agents:
for the USA: Stylus Publishing LLC, PO Box 605, Herndon, VA 20172-0605
tel 800 232 0223; fax 703 661 1501; email styluspub@aol.com
for Canada: Fernwood Books Ltd., PO Box 9409, Stn. A, Halifax, Nova Scotia B3K 5S3
tel 902 422 3302; fax 902 422 3179; email fernwood@istar.ca
for southern Africa: David Philip Publishers, PO Box 23408, Claremont, Cape Town 7735, South Africa
tel +27 (0)21 64 4136; fax +27 (0)21 64 3358; email dpp@iafrica.com
for Australia: Bushbooks, PO Box 1958, Gosford, NSW 2250
tel 02 4323 3274; fax 02 9212 2468; email bushbook@ozemail.com.au

For the rest of the world, contact Oxfam Publishing, 274 Banbury Road, Oxford OX2 7DZ, UK.
tel + 44 (0)1865 311311; fax + 44 (0)1865 313925; email publish@oxfam.org.uk

Published by Oxfam GB
274 Banbury Road, Oxford OX2 7DZ, UK
(registered as a charity, no. 202918)

Designed and typeset by Oxfam Design Department
Printed by Oxfam Print Unit

Oxfam GB is a member of Oxfam International.

Contents

Contents

Acknowledgements

The authors would like to thank all those in Ghana who contributed to the research on which this paper is based, and especially Isaac Osei, of ActionAid. Thanks are due also to all those in Oxford, especially the staff of the Oxfam Gender and Learning Team and the West Africa Desk, for their support while it was being written. Above all, we thank Ben Pugansoa, Programme Manager for Oxfam GB in Ghana, for his assistance and encouragement throughout the whole process.

Ada van der Linde
Rachel Naylor
October 1998

Acronyms and glossary

acephalous: segmentary society with no chiefs or other secular political leaders

ADD: Action on Disability and Development

AGDRS: Assemblies of God Development and Relief Services

BADECC: Business Advisory Development and Consultancy Centre

cephalous: society with chiefs as part of its political structure

CRS: Catholic Relief Services

DAYA: Dagomba Youth Association

DCE: District Chief Executive

enskinment: process of installation of a chief

gate: one of the family lines designated to propose candidates for chiefship

KOYA: Konkomba Youth Association

MoFA: Ministry of Food and Agriculture

NAYA: Nanumba Youth Association

NORYDAL: Northern Region Youth and Development Association

NPI: Nairobi Peace Initiative (Kenyan NGO)

ODA: UK Overseas Development Administration (now Department for International Development)

PAC: Peace Awareness Committee

paramountcy: paramount chieftaincy, supreme authority

PPNT: Permanent Peace Negotiation Team (government-appointed)

REGSEC: Regional Security Council

TIDA: Ti Yum Taaba Development Association

WFP: World Food Programme

Currency: 1 billion cedis = 1 million US$ (1994)

1 Executive summary

Background to the conflict

When communities lose their stakes in peace, conflict breaks out. The reasons behind civil war in Africa are often connected with livelihoods and power. Tensions may centre on ethnic differences and other identities. There are also always issues specific to particular contexts. The main causes of the 1994–5 conflict in northern Ghana are summarised below.

Economic insecurity and uneven development

• Northern Ghana remains a relatively undeveloped area. Public-service provision is weak, standards of literacy, nutrition, and health are correspondingly poor, and agriculture undeveloped. This situation creates insecurity. It has been exacerbated by the negative impacts of economic structural adjustment.

• Within the region, some areas are particularly deprived in terms of service infrastructure, especially the rural areas. This disproportionately affects the ethnic groups concentrated in those areas, often acephalous populations (segmentary groups or groups without chiefs), and this in turn heightens tensions between ethnic groups.

Disputes centred on land and production issues

• Access to land and rights of control over land use are contested between different ethnic groups. 'Chiefly' (cephalous) groups claim ultimate ownership of land, vested in paramount chiefs. Acephalous peoples (with no chiefly power structures) contest this.

• Production systems differ. Acephalous groups tend to practise long-term shifting cultivation, moving on to fertile areas when soil fertility is exhausted. Cephalous groups tend to live in permanent nucleated villages, using a system of rotational fallowing to maintain soil fertility. This has led to tension where cephalous groups believe 'their' land to be damaged by shifting cultivation practices.

• Outright land sales are few. Most land is controlled by traditional authorities. Which authority has this right in any particular area may be contested. State-registered land titling is possible, but remains restricted.

• Limited agricultural development has prioritised rice. Funds have been available for large-scale entrepreneurs to create irrigated rice farms. They have sometimes purchased land titles outright, using their knowledge of the formal land-titling processes. This has created tensions in these areas where local farmers consider that their rights to land have been trespassed upon.

• Competition in the wholesaling and retailing of yams has created tensions. Markets have also become symbolically important in terms of ethnic identity, and practically significant as arenas for meeting and organising for war. The Konkomba yam market in Accra is a case in point.

Issues of governance

• There have been disputes over traditional political leadership in the Northern Region, where four chiefly groups claim the right to rule. In terms of numbers, these groups are in the minority. The 12 acephalous groups now claim the right to self-determination. The denial of this right has precipitated conflict.

A further cause of conflict is the fact that chiefly groups have paramount chiefs who wield great influence over development and decide on traditional questions and land matters, co-operating on these issues as members of the Houses of Chiefs. Acephalous groups also seek self-determination in the form of chieftaincy structures and aspire to have their own paramounts, in order to influence the course of development and to gain representation and sway in the Regional and National Houses of Chiefs.

• Tensions have arisen from the democratisation and decentralisation processes: recent initiatives have opened up competition for limited resources at the local level. Where District authorities have become the preserve of one ethnic group, manipulation of resource-flows by that group has sometimes disadvantaged others.

7

• The rise of youth associations has been a cause of conflict. With the spread of education, associations have been formed, headed by members of the literate urban elite. These constitute an alternative power base to chieftaincy in the Region. At first working for the development of the Region and for education in particular, newer associations have been formed along ethnic lines and they work for these smaller group interests. Since ethnic groups are effectively in competition (for the limited state resources in the Region, land control, and so on), these groups are often mutually hostile. Alliances tend to form within groupings of the traditionally cephalous and groupings of acephalous youth associations. Youth associations as well-established structures have been implicated in inciting conflict in pursuit of their own interests.

Religious identity

• In rural areas, cults of the earth are practised, and there have been disputes over who has the right to perform associated rituals. These are often disputes between cephalous and acephalous peoples.

• Most Muslims in northern Ghana belong to chiefly ethnic groups, whereas most Christians are members of acephalous societies. Tensions between these groups have been fuelled by partisan missionary and development organisations, deciding to assist one group and not another.

Ethnicity

• Some development work has empowered certain groups to assert their ethnic identities and even to crystallise and standardise identities that were previously disparate.

• The ethnic groups make conflicting claims about rights to particular areas of land, based on contrasting legitimising factors (conquest or claims to an indigenous origin). These are linked to claims about rights either to rule other groups or to gain independence from such rule.

The arms race

Although weapons of war have been officially banned in northern Ghana since 1981, arms were stockpiled and other preparations were made before the 1994–5 conflict. This exacerbated tensions.

Previous conflicts

Northern Ghana has been subject to a cycle of conflict. Previously unresolved issues and desire for revenge form the background to this conflict. Rising belligerence, fuelled by rumours and the press and by partial application of justice and day-to-day insults, served to increase tensions.

Dispute over a guinea fowl

Conflict was generally expected six months before its outbreak, although not on the scale on which it actually occurred. The spark for the war was a dispute over the price of a guinea fowl at a market in the Nanumba District.

The impact of the conflict

• The conflict affected seven Districts in the Northern Region. Both modern weaponry and traditional techniques were used. Fighting was most intense between February and May 1994 and in March 1995.

• Lives lost are estimated at 15,000. Approximately 200,000 people were displaced.

• The conflict entailed destruction of personal property, housing, and government services and infrastructure, and the dislocation of social life.

• Interruption of the agricultural cycle meant food shortages throughout the country. Vast government expenditure on peace-keeping reduced development budgets.

Immediate peace-keeping and humanitarian response

• Government peace-keeping was effective and fair and has received wide acclaim.

• The government undertook a relief and rehabilitation programme, including a refugee evacuation and shelter programme, with food-aid assistance from the WFP.

• Non-government organisations (NGOs) in northern Ghana formed an informal Consortium which co-ordinated their humanitarian aid efforts. NGOs organised refugee camps, food distributions, and the provision of other basic necessities. Co-operation with government peace-keepers and relief efforts was good.

The peace process

Government

• The government formed a Permanent Peace Negotiating Team that negotiated with each of the warring factions separately to draft a peace treaty in June 1994. This initiative had limited long-term success in terms of reconciliation, because the parties were not brought together, and the approach relied on arbitration rather than facilitation.

NGOs and civil society

• Seeing that NGO efforts at long-term development were being compromised by recurrent conflict in the Region, the Consortium sought permission to complement government efforts through a parallel peace process.

• The Consortium sought the co-operation of the Nairobi Peace Initiative (NPI), a Kenyan NGO specialising in conciliation work.

• The Consortium and NPI started work at the grassroots, seeking to build up trust with communities and at the same time seek out peace-makers who could head a peace and reconciliation process led by representatives of civil society.

• After identifying such 'voices of reason' among all the warring factions, the Consortium and NPI went on to facilitate peace workshops with all these individuals together at Kumasi. A civil-society organising group, the Peace Awareness Committee, was then formed. It worked with the Consortium and the NPI to continue peace education work at the local, Regional, and national levels and to facilitate more workshops at Kumasi involving various influential actors in the north, from youth-association leaders to politicians.

• The talks were highly successful: tensions eased, and some of the bases of the conflict were addressed. The process resulted in the signing of the Kumasi Peace Accord by the warring factions in March 1996.

• The peace process also entailed the creation and capacity-building of a new body, the Northern Region Youth and Development Association (NORYDA). Its Constitution was ratified by leaders of 12 ethnic groups in the Region. As a representative civil-society organisation, it aims to continue the peace campaign, defuse new tensions that arise, and work for the development of the Region. It provides the capacity for northern peoples to solve their own problems together, to sustain the peace process.

• Since the creation of NORYDA, the body has assisted in the dispersion of tension in the Region on several occasions. NORYDA provides means for creating sustainable peace.

• Peace-awareness groups, meetings, and working groups for peace were established to work on the issues in the communities. This work is being continued and co-ordinated by NORYDA.

• Some of the contested issues have been resolved. For example, chiefly groups have agreed to recognise new paramount chiefs of some of the traditionally acephalous groups. Other issues remain outstanding, notably the Nawuri–Gonja land-ownership dispute, which has been exacerbated by tensions over the distribution of food aid during the current food crisis.

Conclusion

• NGO networks, like the Consortium, can play an invaluable role in promoting a sustainable peace after conflict. Networks provide a neutral status which allows NGOs to work with groups across civil society.

• Informal, flexible consortia have many advantages. In northern Ghana, an informal consortium has been created which can build on its capacities generated during the conflict response, and its flexibility, to take on other roles. Indeed it is attempting to do this during the current food crisis in north-east Ghana.

• The process is a good example of the advantages that can be gained by networking with other specialised NGOs in the continent to share skills and build learning and capacities.

• In working towards the creation of a strong civil-society organisation and in continuing to fund it, capacity can be built within civil society to modify relationships peaceably and to sustain peace.

Summary of recommendations

For the Consortium

Organisation and direction: Retain the flexible character of the Consortium. Build its capacity by devising emergency-preparedness plans, incorporating more gender planning, improving co-ordination, fostering linkages with international donors, and strengthening relations with local and national government to improve collaboration on information-sharing and other responses to conflict.

Consortium activities: Continue to support NORYDA. Institute peace training with NGOs, government officials, and local leaders. Implement data-gathering and disseminating for early warning on crises.

Individual NGOs: Incorporate peace objectives into development work, and monitor on this basis. Improve development planning with government at all levels and with other NGOs. Many NGOs need to build capacities for all these areas.

For local government

Continue to promote peace and improve the impartiality of resource distribution. Improve collaboration with NGOs.

For traditional authority and civil-society leaders

Build on reconciliation work at all levels and adhere to the Kumasi Peace Accord. Improve collaboration with local government, especially in the development of political representation for all groups. Support and increase the capacity of NORYDA. The Houses of Chiefs should work to improve the representative capacity of these institutions and work quickly on conflict-related issues concerning chieftaincy and land.

For central government

Continue the successful peace-keeping efforts. Ensure that policy incorporates development for all, to address inter-Regional and intra-Regional imbalances. Facilitate political participation for all. Tighten arms-control measures. Recognise and support NORYDA's work and NGO development activity.

For donors

Lobby for and support the equitable development of the Northern Region. Assist NORYDA's capacity-building and peace and development work. Support the Consortium's future activities. Research and recognise the problems of channelling aid through the NGO or government sectors.

2 Introduction

In Northern Ghana, ethnic conflict during 1994 and 1995 resulted in casualties and displacement on an unprecedented scale. NGOs in the region formed a consortium to deal with the immediate crisis and to initiate a process of peace negotiation among the warring factions.

This report describes these events and reviews the peace process. Commissioned by the Consortium, it is based on an analysis of primary and secondary documents in Ghana and the UK, undertaken by Ada van der Linde and Rachel Naylor, and on interviews carried out in Ghana in August and September 1996 by Ada van der Linde and in October 1998 by Rachel Naylor.

Interview respondents comprised the following:

- Leaders of the warring factions who participated in NGO-sponsored peace workshops and agreements: chiefs, youth association leaders, opinion leaders, and members of Parliament.

- Principal representatives of the NGO Consortium.
- Government officials at Regional and District levels.
- Divisional chiefs, community leaders, and men and women at village level.
- Aid-agency representatives based in Accra.

The initiative for this documentation came from non-government organisations. Consequently, there was limited access to government officials at national and local level. Van der Linde could not meet with the government-appointed Permanent Peace Negotiation Team (PPNT). Thus, the report says little about the government perspective.

This final report was written by Rachel Naylor.

3 Background to the conflict

Introduction

Political and economic overview

Northern Ghana comprises three Regions: Northern, Upper East, and Upper West, bordered by Togo, Côte d'Ivoire, and Brong Ahafo Region (Figure 1). Together, these three Regions constitute one third of Ghana's land area. The 1994–5 conflict was confined to the Northern Region.

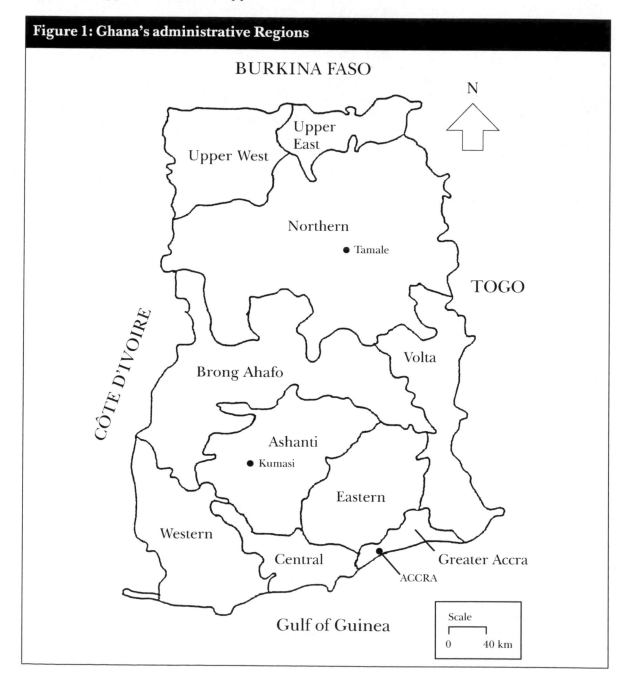

Figure 1: Ghana's administrative Regions

Before independence, northern Ghana was administered as a separate Protectorate by the British. Independence in 1957 brought unity and a promising economic start. However, strong state intervention in the economy, coupled with a policy of import-substituting industrialisation and agricultural mechanisation, resulted in a sharp economic decline that began in 1975. By 1983 the country was in crisis. This led to the adoption of economic liberalisation and structural adjustment policies in conjunction with the IMF and the World Bank, and a certain level of economic recovery.

The macro-economy grew 50 per cent during 1983–93, and Ghana was hailed as a flagship of economic reform by the IMF.[1] However, the social impact of the reforms has been severe. Adjustment involved thousands of compulsory redundancies in the civil service and the parastatal organisations. Cost-recovery was introduced in health and education services, resulting in sharp declines in attendance at health centres and schools. Removal of agricultural subsidies meant that inputs rose drastically in price, affecting production. These changes had the greatest impact on the poor.

Under-development and uneven development in Ghana

Northern Ghana has a harsh environment with a single, unpredictable period of rainfall each year (southern Ghana has two) and poor soils. Under colonial rule, different policies (relating to education, agriculture, law, and so on) were applied to northern Ghana. What comparative advantages the area might have had, in terms of potential for cotton and shea-nut production, for example, were not exploited. This resulted in the under-development of this area in comparison with the rest of the country. Since policy was implemented through chiefs, under the system known as 'Indirect Rule', this also led to uneven development, often favouring some groups (with chiefs) over others. To a certain extent, this pattern has continued ever since.

According to analysis of the Ghana Living Standards Survey, 54 per cent of the poorest 10 per cent live in the north, although the north accounts for only 25 per cent of the total population.[2] However, the north is an area of low government spending. For example, the Northern Region accounts for 15 per cent of the population, yet only 5 per cent of national resources are spent here.[3] As a result, the north is

an area of out-migration. As this migration involves more men than women, women who are left behind face increased burdens as they take on some of the men's work in addition to their own.[4]

Education

Education suffered during the economic decline, as fewer teachers were trained, school infrastructure deteriorated, and enrolment rates fell. Rural schools were harder hit than urban institutions, and girls were more affected than boys.

In the north, educational provision is particularly poor, except in the major District capitals.[5] Although cost-recovery in the form of user-fees in education has not been introduced in this area, because of its poverty, levies for Parent–Teacher Associations and other dues are still enough to deter many parents from sending their children to school. Enrolment rates are much higher in the south. Illiteracy rates in the north are 92 per cent for women and 70 per cent for men, while the national averages are 64 per cent and 38 per cent.[6] Literacy rates tend to be worse among ethnic groups living predominantly in rural areas, particularly the Konkomba. Education is the principal means of wealth acquisition and social differentiation in the north.[7] These inequalities of educational opportunity create a basis for ethnic strife in the north.

Health

Economic decline also took its toll on government health-service provision, and user fees have deterred attendance at clinics and hospitals.

Health status and infrastructure are generally poorer in the north than elsewhere in Ghana. NGO provision is generally of excellent quality but limited; government provision is scarce. Health care is especially weak in the rural areas. Predominantly rural groups, particularly the Konkomba, suffer from this pattern of provision.

Severe nutritional deficiencies are common in the rural north, even in ordinary years, especially during the 'hunger season' before the first harvest of the year. This is a source of tension.

Agriculture

The north's principal crops are food crops: yam, maize, guinea corn, millet, groundnuts, and cowpeas. It also produces rice, shea nuts (mostly gathered from wild trees), and cotton for cash and export. However, the main emphasis in national policy implementation remains (as in the colonial era) on the southern export-crop sector: cocoa, coffee, and palm oil. Development support for food crops is relatively small. This means that northern farmers tend to be poorer than those in the south.

Under structural adjustment, subsidies for fertiliser, seeds, and traditional agricultural technologies (hoes, cutlasses, and sacks) were withdrawn. This has affected the north particularly badly. There has been a significant

fall in northern maize and rice production in favour of yam, groundnuts, and millet, which do not require fertiliser.

In the north, post-adjustment agricultural schemes such as the Low Risk Agriculture Project[8] and Global 2000[9] are of limited benefit. However, the newly liberalised cotton sector, working with cotton outgrowers, offers increasing opportunities for small-scale farmers to benefit from fertilisers, insecticides, and tractor-ploughing.

Figure 2: Major ethnic groups in northern Ghana (reproduced with the permission of the publisher from Barker 1986)

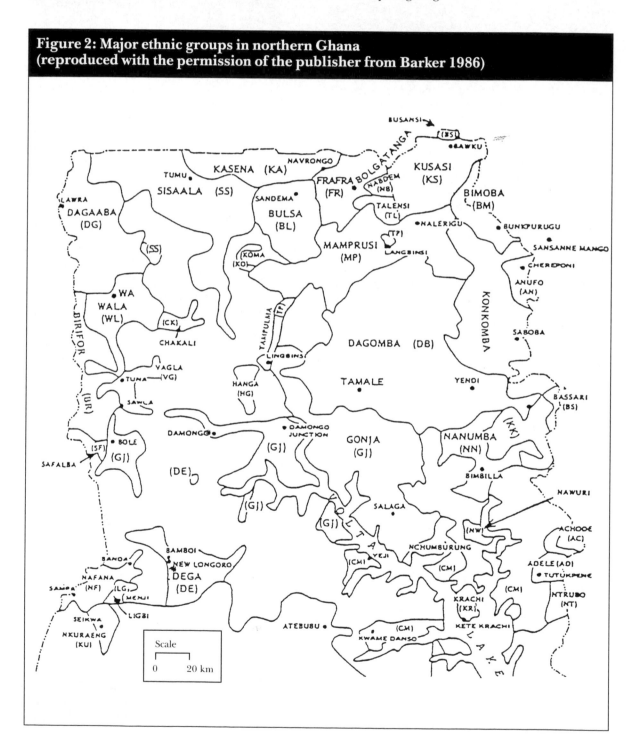

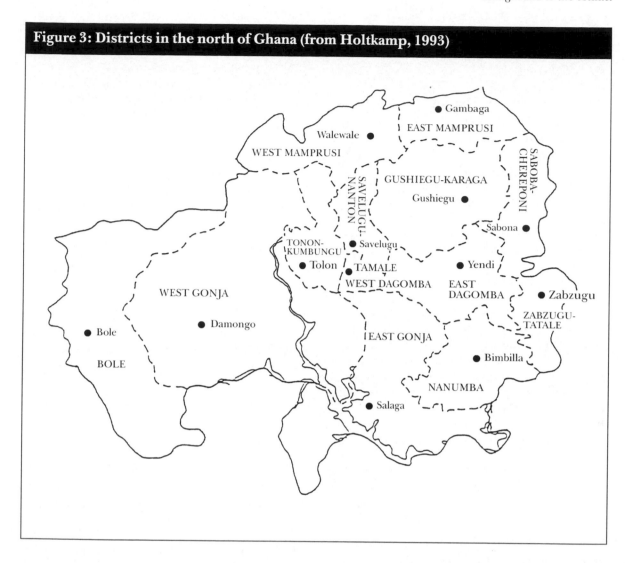

Figure 3: Districts in the north of Ghana (from Holtkamp, 1993)

Population and ethnic groups in the Northern Region

There are 16 major ethnic groups in the Northern Region.[10] Ten are traditionally acephalous:[11] Anufo, Bassare, Bimoba, Builsa, Konkomba, Mo, Nawuri, Nchumuru, Tampollensi, and Vagala. Four are cephalous: Dagomba, Gonja, Mamprusi, and Nanumba. Figure 2 indicates the principal geographical areas of each ethnic group in the Northern Region. Since many of the group members are spread throughout the Region, live in multi-ethnic settlements, and inter-marry, this is only a guide.

The population of the Northern Region is estimated at 1.44 million, mostly living in 3,000 scattered settlements. This makes it the most sparsely populated Region, with a density of 20 per square kilometre.[12] Notably, the areas where fighting was most intense in 1994–5

(Yendi, Saboba, Chereponi, Salaga) are areas of relatively low population density.

The latest population figures from the last Census (1994) do not disaggregate the Region by ethnic groups. Estimates suggest that the 1994 populations of the largest groups involved in the conflict were Dagombas 268,000, Konkombas 247,000, Gonjas 134,000, and Nanumbas 27,000.[13] The numerical strength of the Konkombas suggested by these figures is striking in the light of assertions that acephalous groups are 'minority' groups, a claim sometimes used to justify the lack of representation afforded to acephalous groups by traditional politics. Given that large groups, such as the Konkombas, or groups which are numerically dominant in certain areas, such as the Nawuris at Kpandai or the Konkombas in the Nanumba District, must pay allegiance to smaller ruling groups, tensions and demands for self-determination are not surprising.

Land, production, and settlement

Land and state legislation

Since 1902 the colonial and post-colonial states have enacted various land laws. Some of them have vested land in the state rather than the chiefs, and some have attempted to regulate land use and register land 'ownership'.[14] The most significant impact of this was that during the colonial era large-scale land sales were prevented. This pre-empted the emergence of a land market, unlike in the south of Ghana.

In practice, most land has remained outside the regulation of the state, because the use and implementation of formal land law and registration procedures has been limited. The current Constitution (Republic of Ghana 1992) vests land in chiefs.

Chiefly control of land has not traditionally implied private ownership in the Western sense. Land ownership has been bound up with the political power to control *people* within an area, rather than control over *territory*. Kingdoms were based on the control of people (a scarce economic resource) rather than land (which was plentiful).[15] However, by the late 1970s, chiefly domination had increasingly come to mean territorial control in some areas. This position was bolstered by the 1979 Constitution.[16]

The Third Republic ... for the first time in the modern history of Ghana recognised that land tenure is vested in the ethnic groups and their authorities which happen to be historically dominant in any particular area.

This conceptual shift to viewing land as privately owned in some areas has also been exacerbated by the increasing value of land (particularly its reconstitution as scarce building land in urban areas and as a scarce productive resource in rice-growing areas) and by changes in production relations (see below).

Formal land sales

Formal land acquisition remains limited. It is confined to the sales of plots in urban areas for housing, and for state and business use[17] (such as government buildings from hospitals to administrative blocks, and company premises), government acquisition of land in rural areas for various projects (such as agricultural stations, air-strips, forest and wildlife reserves, military uses), and the private purchase of rural land (principally for rice farms and NGO agricultural projects).

Land control and acquisition at the local level

Although the 'ultimate' title to land is recognised by the state as vested in chiefs, land at the local level is regarded as 'owned' (controlled) by lineages (family lines or 'clans'). All land is regarded as owned by someone.

Most rural land is never sold. When 'strangers' require land, they will make a request to the head of a lineage, at the same time as presenting 'kola' (which is often actual kola nuts or another token gift). If there is spare land, the landowner will lend it. The landowner may take the land back after a year, but long-term land lending is common. The borrower may offer part of his or her harvest to the owner, but this is not a requirement.

The ultimate source of tension here is over land ownership. For acephalous groups to acquire land, they are required to participate in a process which recognises that the land belongs to others.

Production and settlement

Most farmers operate on a small-scale, semi-subsistence basis. Production patterns vary according to ethnic group. Chiefly groups tend to live in nucleated villages and farm on the perimeters of the village, using a crop-rotation and fallowing system. Acephalous groups, particularly Konkombas, often live on isolated farmsteads which are scattered across the landscape. When soil fertility is reduced in one area, acephalous people move on to a new one, which results in patterns of long-distance migration over the generations. Political factors invariably affect the direction of this movement. For example, Skalnik (1983) describes the mass migration of Konkombas into the Nanumba area in colonial times, caused by the 'pull' of fertile soil and the 'push' of the relatively more coercive colonial practices in Togo.

The different production systems are a source of tension. For example, Konkomba farming practices are criticised by chiefly groups, who claim that Konkomba will farm land until it is exhausted and then move on, leaving poor land. Migrations are also a source of tension when they occur on a large scale.

Marketing

Ethnic conflict in 1981 saw a change in marketing patterns. Konkomba practise extensive yam cultivation; until that point they were marketing through Nanumba middlemen. They then began to market their own produce, and this led to the development of the Konkomba yam market in Accra.

Some interviewees noted that this switch in marketing has led to ethnic tension. Certainly, the Konkomba market in Accra became a focus for the articulation of Konkomba identity, and, later on, a forum in which to organise and to raise money for the 1994–5 struggle.

The consequences of new production developments for land

In contrast with the south, there is little extensive agricultural development in northern Ghana. Larger-scale rice projects are the exception to this.

In the 1970s, Ghanaian and German development aid contributed to the development of irrigated rice farming and upland rice farming on natural swamps. The huge Ghanaian-German Agricultural Development Programme (GGDAP) intensified mechanised farming and exacerbated deforestation, particularly in the Northern Region. The programme sought to draw the Region into the global rice market.

Anxious to protect long-term investments in irrigation and equipment, some rice entrepreneurs bought the land from chiefs and used their knowledge of the formal sector to register the purchases. This created conflicts in areas where the original population felt dispossessed, and they denied that the chiefs had the right to sell the land. This has even led to incidents of rice-burning and acts of vandalism against rice machinery.[18]

Some changing production relations, then, have been a source of conflict in northern Ghana.

Governance

The nation state, democratisation, and decentralisation

After 11 years of military rule, democratisation at the national level began with the 1992 multiparty presidential and parliamentary elections. Jerry Rawlings was elected as President of the new Fourth Republic in 1992 and re-elected in 1996. One source of tension arising from the parliamentary system is that MPs often lobby for the development of their own areas and ethnic groups. Under-represented groups are at a disadvantage.

Ghana is divided into 10 Regions and 110 Districts. The Northern Region comprises 10 Districts. There are no Regional democratic forums, but Districts were democratised in 1989. One third of the District Assembly members are elected. Democratisation at a lower level, the Unit, is currently underway. Democratisation is at its early stages, since decision-making is still largely centralised.

Administrative decentralisation is also being carried out at Regional and District levels. Regional Ministers and Regional Administrations co-ordinate activities of the sector ministries at that level and liaise with the NGO sector. There are also Regional-level Security Councils (REGSECs). The newest tier of administrative decentralisation is the District Administration (with District Chief Executives as politically appointed heads, and District Co-ordinating Directors as government bureaucratic heads, with their sectoral district officers), which co-ordinates District-level ministry activity.

There are sometimes tensions between District Chief Executives and District Co-ordinating Directors as political interests and intrigues come into play.

The District Assemblies draw up District Development Plans and Budgets. The District Assembly has access to funds to pay for the Plans from the government-allocated District Assemblies' Common Fund. Since 5 per cent of this Fund must be raised locally, it is evident that Assemblies in more prosperous urban and rural areas benefit most from this system. It is much harder for District Assemblies to raise income locally in the north. Consequently, better services, paid for by the Common Fund, can be provided in the south.[19]

In practice, the use of budgets is often subject to manipulation for vote-winning and aggrandisement of those in power. Budget allocations are still influenced by Accra and by the dominant ethnic groups in the District Assembly, leading to uneven development. The new possibilities created by this innovation — the access to decision-making, power and resources — partly explain why groups struggle for representation or indeed a District of their own, where the existing District Assembly does not seem to provide for their needs. Holtkamp (1993:290) notes that decentralisation has led to the sharpening of ethnic conflicts in many Districts throughout Ghana.

'Traditional' political organisation

Forms of traditional political organisation are very strong in Ghana. Political organisation often takes the form of hierarchical chieftaincy structures operating in centralised traditional states. Paramount chiefs are at the pinnacle of these structures, with responsibility for installing divisional chiefs, who in turn install lesser chiefs. Eligibility to compete for chiefship is ascribed through inherited membership of particular lineages.[20] In the north, unlike most of Ghana, chiefs cannot be relieved of their positions. Today, Traditional Councils act as secretariats for paramount chiefs and are consulted in traditional matters.

In the Northern Region, the four chiefly groups are regarded as descendants of a small band of invaders who entered the region approximately 400 years ago. Traditionally, these chiefs have been able to call on warrior lineages to mobilise for war. Today, they regard themselves as ruling over members of the cephalous and acephalous groups within the 'orbits' of their chiefship.[21] This position was bolstered in colonial times, when the British ruled through chiefs under the indirect-rule policy.[22] The geographical areas to which the orbits correspond have waxed and waned over the years, according to the strength of the chiefly groups and the power of acephalous groups at the periphery to resist rule. In the context of the nation state they are loosely demarcated and labelled Traditional Areas. Figure 4 shows these capitals and other principal towns in Northern Region.

Some acephalous groups claim to be indigenous to the area. Other acephalous groups claim to be settlers in the area. Traditionally segmentary in structure,[23] these groups are not centralised and may be composed of many sub-groups scattered over a wide area. For example, the Konkomba are composed of 17 clans living in several Districts within and outside the Region and in Togo. The Nchumurus are also spread over five Districts, within and outside the Region. This reflects the pattern of production and migration described. In other cases, acephalous groups are confined to one region, for example the Nawuri, who consider themselves as indigenous to the Kpandai area.

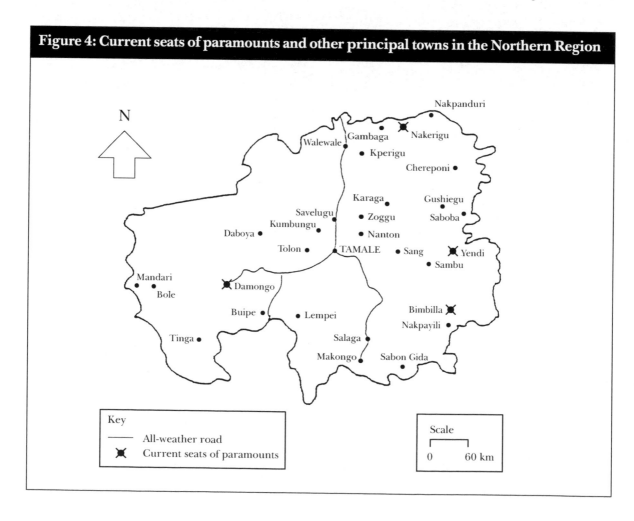

Figure 4: Current seats of paramounts and other principal towns in the Northern Region

Konkombas are a significant acephalous group within the Dagomba, Gonja, and Nanumba orbits of chiefship. Nawuris and Nchumurus live within the Gonja orbit. The legitimacy of chiefly rule is questioned by all these groups. Concurrence with chiefly rule has involved paying allegiance to chiefs through respecting traditional ceremonies, accepting chiefly authority in all manner of disputes from land to marriage, following customary codes of conduct, and making symbolic gifts at various times, such as after hunting game.[24] These vary according to the chiefly group. How far chiefly groups can impose their will, and how far acephalous groups co-operate with custom and demand, determine the nature of allegiance paid at any one time.

Chiefs and people from chiefly societies are represented in the Regional and National Houses of Chiefs by paramount chiefs. In the Northern House of Chiefs, for example, the four chiefly groups are represented. This cannot constitute a quorum.

The sphere of action of the Houses is over Chieftaincy matters and land disputes. In the north, land is vested in chiefs under the 1992 Constitution. Given the importance of chieftaincy in everyday life and the significance of land, direct representation in these Houses is now sought after by all ethnic groups. This is a significant cause of conflict. Current chieftaincy structures in the Northern Region are represented in Table 1.

Table 2 presents the acephalous groups currently demanding chieftaincy in order to benefit from representation in the Northern House of Chiefs. As one report[26] noted, the 'process of elevation to Paramountcy ... has now become a yardstick for social and even political strength among various ethnic groups'.

Table 2: Acephalous groups claiming chieftaincy

Ethnic group	Konkomba	Nchumuru	Nawuri
Kingdom/ capital claim[27]	Saboba		Kpandai
Paramount chiefship claim	Ucha-bobor	Nanjirowura	Ubo

Chiefship, local and national government, and development

Apart from their authority over chieftaincy and land matters, chiefs have great influence over many other areas of development. They have particular sway in decision-making and resource-flows in the District.[28] This explains demands for chiefs by acephalous groups and is another source of tension.

Exclusion of members of acephalous ethnic groups from participation in the political process and enjoyment of the fruits of development also extends to non-royal, non-elite members of the chiefly groups. This is a further source of tension.

Youth associations

A Northern Youth Association was set up in the 1960s. It aimed to represent Northern Ghana and promote northerners' interests, especially in education. As education became more widespread, the need for this association lessened.

Newer on the scene, local (often ethnic-based) youth associations have been created over the last few decades.

Table 1: Chieftaincy in the Northern Region

Ethnic group	Dagomba	Gonja	Nanumba	Mamprusi
Kingdom	Dagbon	Gonja	Nanun	Mamprugu
Capital[25]	Yendi	Damongo	Bimbilla	Nalerigu
Paramount title	Ya-Na and his sister Gundulanaa	Yagbonwura	Chambanaa	Nayiri
Divisional chiefs	Mion Lana, Susonaa, Gushienaa	Tulewura, Mandarewura, Kanjasewura	Juonaa, Gambugnaa, Janjirinaa	Soo Naa, Wulugu Naa Yunyorana, Wu-Naa

19

They are voluntary organisations with ascribed membership based on origin in a particular territory or ethnic affiliation. The associations fall together with the definitions of 'traditional areas' or chiefdoms, and the term 'youth' generally implies no age limit on members but is rather a socio-political category which places the associations in the communal framework of the 'chiefs', 'elders' and 'people'. 'Youth' means the politically active who consider themselves opinion leaders, but only in the widest sense does it also mean biologically 'young' men. The ideology and chief activities of the associations are indeed in most cases entirely focused on men, even though women sometimes organise their own parallel meetings. (Lentz, 1995: 395)

Leadership is held by a new literate elite, whose members have attained their position through new forms of social differentiation based on education.[29] They act to conscientise and empower their ethnic groups. As Lentz (1995: 395) notes, the leaders have increasingly 'acted as spokesmen of their ethnic groups in the militant ethnic conflicts that have repeatedly shaken the region since the 1970s'. Thus, the importance of youth leaders in terms of political leadership has increased in relation to that of chiefs. Respondents said that youth associations are particularly strong among acephalous groups, particularly the Konkombas.

The principal youth associations in Northern Ghana are the Anufo Progressive Union, Bimoba Youth Association, Dagbon Youth Association, Gonja Youth Association, Konkomba Youth Association, Mamprusi Youth Association, Nanumba Youth Association, Nawuri Youth Association, Nchumuru Youth Association, Tampulma Youth Association, and Vagla Youth Association.

Elite echelons within youth associations were regarded by interview respondents as having an important role in bringing about the 1994–5 conflict.

Ethnicity and identity

Religion and identity

Traditional religion featuring cults of people (ancestor cults, individual shrines) and cults of place (earth cults) remains important in the Northern Region among all ethnic groups. Earth priests have traditionally propitiated the spirits of the land, although observers note that their influence is waning. Since earth priests are regarded as descendants of the first people to clear the virgin bush in an area, rights to propitiate are bound up with claims about ritual stewardship and rights to use land. The right to propitiate has sometimes been a source of conflict in northern Ghana. In Nanun, for example, Nanumba say that only the priests whom they recognise can perform land rites. This right is disputed by the Konkomba earth priests not recognised by the Nanumbas.

Christianity and Islam also find expression here. There are numerous missions, churches, and associated development organisations and projects. Much Christian missionary activity is concentrated among acephalous people, and the number of converts is higher than among cephalous groups. This activity includes running churches, schools, and literacy programmes. Observers note that this work has contributed to the construction of ethnic identities and empowerment, as has the work of some Christian development organisations whose main focus is development or education rather than conversion. For example, Skalnik (1987:307–8) notes for the Konkomba:

... the 'tribe' has emerged only very recently ... They were originally divided into a number of 'sub-tribes'... Likpokpaln (the Konkomba language) is the result of efforts ... of the Ghana Institute of Linguistics, Literacy and Bible Translation, who designed its alphabet, formalised its grammar and published the first textbooks on the basis of the most central Sanguli dialect. The Konkomba speak various, only marginally mutually intelligible dialects. Implicitly this contributes to identity formation.

World Vision, for example, works mainly in Konkomba areas, regarding these regions as particularly impoverished. Empowering the poor and contributing to identity formation in this area may have contributed to conflict. This, of course, is one of the dilemmas of development. However, there have been accusations that some religious organisations have deliberately incited conflict in an effort to address the power imbalance.

Elites of the ruling groups, on the other hand, are generally Islamic.[30] Islamic development agencies are now increasingly supporting the creation of primary schools and the promotion of education as well. Again, this contributes to empowerment and the crystallisation of identities.

Tension related to this religious-ethnic division has grown significantly in the north, with the rise of Christian and Islamic militancy associated with the influx of certain missions in the last 15 years.

Militants constitute a tiny minority. Indeed, numbers of practising Muslims and Christians still remain low. Barker (1986) notes, for example, that only 6 per cent of Konkombas are Christian and only 5 per cent of Nanumbas are Islamic, whereas 2 per cent are Christian. Dagombas are the most Islamicised group: 50 per cent are practising adherents. Even then, most people claiming a religious affiliation still tend to practise an eclectic mix of spiritual activity. However, interviewees stated that, used as a political tool, religious differences have been an important cause of conflict.

Perspectives of the groups[31]

The varied and sometimes conflicting perspectives of the principal groups involved in the 1994–5 conflict, put forward by interviewees, are presented here. These accounts outline the histories, myths, and lived realities which are drawn on to validate contemporary claims to land, sovereignty, and so on, and led to the conflict.

The Gonja perspective

Gonja interviewees claimed that the Gonja chiefly dynasty began with a warrior leader who came from the north-west hundreds of years ago. He fought the settled population and took over the land, corresponding to half of Northern Region. Current boundaries are Kintampo (south), the border with Côte d'Ivoire (west), the area to the east of Kpembe and Kpandai (these areas are included in the claim), and Tamale (north). The Gonja eventually controlled the political situation, but indigenous earth priests were allowed to continue. Some of the indigenous people became warriors in the Gonja army.

Gonja interviewees said that they live with three other ethnic groups in the west and one group (the Nawuris) in the east, with whom they share language and culture (the languages are basically Gonja, although they have a slightly different form).

According to Gonja interview respondents, two recent pre-1994 conflicts involving the Gonja were caused by 'kinsmen' fighting (firstly Gonja and Gonja, then Gonja and Nawuri). A third recent conflict involved the Gonjas against the Konkombas and Nawuris on the other.

Controversial parts of this account include the legitimacy of the political and territorial control claimed by the Gonja, and the assertion that the other ethnic groups do not have distinct languages and identities. These assertions are causes of tension.

The Dagomba perspective

The Dagomba claim to land ownership, and to legal powers over acephalous groups, is based on the fact that Dagombas regard themselves as descendants of an invading chiefly class who defeated indigenous tribes over 400 years ago in the area that is now the Kingdom of Dagbon.

Interviewees said that the Dagomba introduced chieftaincy to the acephalous Konkomba. Konkomba heads and chiefs were gradually recognised by the Dagomba. There had never been discrimination against Konkomba, and this is proved by many inter-marriages. Dagomba interviewees said that over the past 30 years young educated Konkomba have regretted the fact that there is no Konkomba paramount chief. But Konkombas still have chiefs in some areas of Dagbon who pay allegiance to senior Dagomba chiefs.

Konkombas petitioned for paramountcy. Dagombas objected to the way this was done, because it did not respect tradition. In October 1993 and April 1995 the Dagomba Traditional Council denounced the request for paramountcy in writing. 'The carving out of land out of Dagbon for the Saboba-na' was said to be impossible, as the traditions of paramountcy are foreign to Konkombas.

Dagomba interviewees regarded the belligerence of the Konkomba as the cause of the conflict. They believed that the conflict was long-planned. Just before the war, a memorandum saying that Dagbon would be attacked was circulated by Konkombas. Konkombas ceased to pay allegiance to Dagomba chiefs, refusing to give them hind legs of cattle slaughtered at funerals and disregarding the judicial functions of the chiefs.

Respondents also said that Dagbon had not planned for war, and arms had not been stockpiled by Dagombas. Protracted internal chieftaincy problems led in 1981 to an ongoing ban on arms in this area, which the Dagombas respected.

Interviewees also said they felt that the government had tacitly supported the Konkombas. They felt that the problems had been aggravated by Presidential speeches in 1993–4 which suggested that 'the land belongs to no one' and that 'minority' groups should be supported in their requests for land.

This account is controversial in its assertion that Dagomba rule is legitimate, that there has never been anti-Konkomba discrimination, that Saboba land belongs to Dagombas, that Konkomba are the only war-planners and instigators, and that the government had been partisan towards the Konkombas.

The Nanumba perspective

Nanumba interviewees noted that Nanumba people also claim descent from chiefly invaders. Later, under colonialism, Nanumba District was administered as part of German Togoland until 1919, when it was transferred to British administration.

Nanumbas say that they experienced considerable Konkomba migration into the District after World War II as a threat, because it meant that Konkombas could sway things in their favour. However, Nanumba say that they accepted the Konkombas.

Nanumbas lived through severe conflict with Konkombas in 1981, but peace was restored thereafter. Towards 1994, their fear began to increase that Konkombas would try to wipe them out entirely. The creation of the Konkomba Youth Association increased Nanumba fears, as did the mounting refusals of Konkombas to pay allegiance to Nanumba chiefs and submit to their judicial authority. For example, the Konkomba started to refuse to give the cows' hind legs to chiefs at the funerals of important persons, as demanded by tradition.

Nanumba interviewees contended that Konkombas began to receive outside sympathy in the build-up to the war. They also contend that Konkomba have no title to the land and no ambitions for paramountcy. There are 365 self-declared Konkomba 'chiefs', whom Nanumbas do not recognise. Indeed, their creation has caused Nanumbas offence. Nanumbas say that Konkombas did not mix with Nanumbas, because Konkombas felt inferior, and they say that the two groups never intermarried.

The Nanumbas say that they did not expect a war in 1993 and had not planned or prepared for one. There was a build-up of letters, exchanges, accusations, and rumours that led to the conflicts with the other ethnic groups, but the Nanumba did not feel particularly concerned, because they were not mentioned in letters.

Nanumba say that the government acted partially towards the Konkombas. Supporting the Konkombas with housing, the government also gave the impression that 'minority tribes' would gain support if they fought for land. Nanumbas conclude that the Konkombas deliberately caused the war just before the elections, to ensure victory for the Rawlings government.

Nanumba also see some of the Konkomba yam-production and marketing activities to be illegitimate. One respondent commented:

.. land is generally plenty ... So whoever is strong to farm should be allowed to farm. ... But the problem,

one of the things that trigger problems, is the marketing of this produce. Konkombas are the dominant producers of yam. They go to the market and arrange yams in heaps for a particular price. Somebody else goes in to turn them away, and says, 'No you can't do that, you people, you are not from this place. This is our land. You can't come and produce here and sell it at that price.' And it created a lot of friction a number of times. And people fought locally over that.

Controversial parts of this account include the assertion that Nanumbas have a legitimate right to rule over Konkombas, and accusations of Konkomba war-mongering.

The Konkomba perspective

Konkombas claim that they are indigenous to Dagbon. In an interview with *The Ghanaian Times* (1995), 14 Konkomba chiefs claim that long before the Dagomba ancestors set foot in the area 'our forefathers were there, and the Ya-Na's ancestors did not dispossess the Konkomba of their land either through battle or by any other means ...'. Konkomba rather say that they gave sanctuary to the arriving Dagombas. The Konkomba say that Dagomba historians have given the wrong information on land tenure to the Ya-Na. The Dagomba chiefs at Sunsun, Demon, and elsewhere in the Konkomba area are regarded as 'outpost' chiefs by Konkombas. They were sent there to check Konkomba advance and they do not have control over Konkombas.

Konkomba agree that in other areas of Ghana Konkombas are recent settlers and should not have paramountcies. The Konkomba land claim in the Oti Basin is based on long-term settlement. In Nanun, Konkomba settlement is a much more recent phenomenon.

Before the conflict, the Konkombas had petitioned the President for a paramountcy. This had been referred to the Northern Regional House of Chiefs. The demands were for the elevation of the Konkomba Saboba Divisional chief to paramountcy, a Konkomba Traditional council, a Konkomba chief in the Nanumba District, and improved state dealings with Konkombas (including a fair legal process, DCE impartiality towards Konkombas, and an ethnic balance in political appointments). In the petition, the Konkombas threatened that, if they did not get a paramountcy, they would fight for it. Konkombas did not take kindly to the Dagomba refusal of their requests.

Konkomba say that they are disadvantaged by limited access to education and other services.

And with education, people who were considered minorities, they haven't had access to education. So the agitation came that they had to fight for rights and fighting for your rights means they have to make a stand saying: 'Enough is enough of this, we also want to have land'.

Konkombas also say that they have been treated with partiality by chiefs, particularly in the judgement of Konkomba marriage cases. In 1981, Konkombas began to claim and practise the right in Nanumba District to try their own such cases, to avoid embarrassment and promote justice. Coupled with disputes over the right of Nanumba middlemen to dominate the yam trade in the District, this led to the huge Konkomba–Nanumba conflict in 1981.[32] Konkombas also state that they have received derogatory treatment from chiefly groups, being referred to as 'aliens', 'uncivilised people', and so on.

Again, the claims about legitimacy of Konkomba rights to land and self-determination are controversial.

The Nchumuru perspective

The Nchumuru feel that their identity and rights and their claims to Nchumuru land ownership are being denied under Gonja rule. Nchumurus were placed under Gonja rule by the British colonial administration. One interviewee said, 'Until we are identified as groups, we will not participate in anything.' Another said, 'Every Gonjaman knows ... the Nanjirowura, who is the paramount chief of the Nchumurus and who is the aid of Nchumurus in every place ... So, where does the word come from, "Gonja land"?' Nchumurus contest the concept of 'Gonjaland', because it implies that they have no land rights.

Nchumurus state that they feel oppressed in Northern Region. Nchumurus feel they have been discriminated against and that their human identity has been denied. As one interviewee said, 'It is just an evolution. Things have come to a point where people must think that others too are human and they want to live with them as equals.'

They also feel they are denied development. 'We are in five Regions ... [with paramount] chiefs ... [at]Yeji ... Prang ... [and] ... Kpasa. These are all Nchumurus and there is only a small segment of [us] in Northern Region. That is why we are suffering. We have become a minority.'

Nchumurus describe how they tried to bring themselves, Nawuris, and the Gonjas together in 1980, by suggesting a joint youth and development association. However, they claim that the idea was subverted by the Gonjas.

... at that time there were Gonja Youth Association, Nawuri Youth Association, Nchumuru Youth Association, Konkomba Youth Association. So when we met we decided, okay let's just go and find a solution to all this dichotomy. ... so that we will have an all-embracing union that will bring us together and then we will be able to sort of recommend good relationships and resist any tension that we can foresee to be coming. When the Gonjas went for their Gonja Youth Association meeting in Damongo, they came back with this all infuriating terminology: 'Gonjaland Youth Association' ...

Bitterness about the relationship with Gonjas led to Nchumurus and Nawuris fighting Gonjas in 1991. The same unresolved issues led to the 1994 conflict. The legitimacy of the Nchumuru claim to land and political independence is controversial.

The Nawuri perspective

Nawuris assert that they are indigenous to the Kpandai area and claim the land there as Nawuri territory. This is contested by the Gonjas. The status of the area was not clarified under colonial rule. It was first administered as part of German Togoland under Yendi (the Dagomba capital) and then as part of Salaga District by the British. This encouraged Gonja claims, since Salaga is a Gonja town.

The area is administered on paper by the Salaga District Assembly. However, the Nawuris say that educational and health services are being refused to them by a partisan Assembly. (Gonjas claim that it is rather the Nawuris who refuse to accept these services, as it would imply dependence rather than sovereignty.) Nawuris certainly do not want Kpandai to remain under the Salaga District Assembly, arguing that it denies their status. They demand a separate District. Currently, Nawuris use health and education services provided by the World Evangelical Council.

Nawuris have developed chiefs and say that all 'strangers' in Kpandai, among whom they include Gonjas, are acceptable as citizens who respect Nawuri chiefs, and not 'overlords'.

Before 1992, the Nawuris attempted to go through the central government to attain the paramountcy they desired. However, after the 1992 Constitution was put in place, the government said that this document implied that only Houses of Chiefs could decide on chieftaincy matters. The National House of Chiefs did not consider the case, and the Nawuris believed that it would not do so, because they are a small group. This was a further source of tension.

Once more, Nawuris make controversial claims for self-determination.

Table 3: Some recent conflicts in the Northern Region

Year	Groups involved	Description
1981	Konkombas and Nanumbas	Issue: chieftaincy reforms instituted by Konkomba Youth Association. Largest conflict pre-1994.
1984	Bimobas and Konkombas	Issue: chieftaincy. In the north-east of the Region. Sparked by a market dispute. 20 dead.
1986	Bimobas and Konkombas	About 20 dead.
1989	Bimobas and Konkombas	About 20 dead.
1991	Nawuris and Gonjas	Issue: Nawuri independence at Kpandai. Modern weapons used. 78 dead.
	Dagombas	Issue: succession dispute at Karaga and Gushiegu. 40 dead.
	Dagombas and security forces	Issue: anti-government feeling at Tamale. Riot at traditional Fire Festival, 8 dead.
1992	Konkomba, Nawuri, Bassare, Nchumurus and Gonjas	Issue: chieftaincy. High death toll.
	Dagombas and security forces	Issue: post-election anti-government feeling. Riot in Tamale.
1993	Mossis and Konkombas	Issue: chieftaincy. Spilled into Togo.

Previous conflicts and unresolved issues

The 1994–5 conflict followed a cycle of conflict and insecurity in the north of Ghana, related to anti-government disputes, intra-ethnic succession disputes, feuds within ethnic groups, and inter-ethnic disagreements between cephalous and acephalous groups.[33] Recent conflicts are listed in Table 3. Some of the unresolved disputes from these conflicts formed the bones of contention in the 1994–5 war.

Arms race

Preparations for conflict, the stockpiling of weapons, and the availability of arms also contributed to the war. There had been an ongoing government ban on arms for war since 1981, but arms control is difficult to maintain in the context of an under-resourced state and in a situation where weapons are widely used for hunting and at funeral rites.

The 1994 conflict was the first time that modern arms, such as AK47s, were widely used in conflict in the Northern Region. Their origin is not established, but they were certainly widely available. An NGO report[34] on a meeting with the Minister of Employment and Social Welfare states:

Even government admits not to have anticipated the scale and intensity of the fighting, which was unprecedented, and that the conflict had very serious fundamental undertones. Until 1994, similar eruptions had been very localised; but this time there was use of very sophisticated weapons, which exposed the fact that there could be some external factors at play as well.

One interviewee commented:

There were more arms around ... and they were actively sold... in Tamale, Accra, and in other markets. The presence of arms seems to have been a cause or at least a heavily provocative factor in the conflict and in the spread of the violence.

The arms build-up was funded by careful organisation on the part of some of the groups.

Exclusion, subjection, belligerence

Often, chiefly rule involves the exclusion of members of acephalous ethnic groups from participation in the political process and from enjoyment of the fruits of development. It has sometimes gone further than this, entailing oppression. For example, the traditional system allows for flexibility in patterns of land control. Where acephalous people have been staying on land for several years, they can be given permanent land-holding status. To deliberately deny this without good reason, as has so often been the case, according to interviewees, may be regarded as subjection. Another example is the abrupt way in which acephalous petitions for paramountcy have been rejected.

On a day-to-day level, some of the interviewees said that the tensions were raised by individuals from chiefly groups belittling individuals from acephalous groups. No one likes to be made to feel inferior. This everyday situation is a key issue. In the face of these denials of representation, identity, and status, acephalous groups have demanded self-determination.

On the other hand, animosity and belligerence have also been shown by acephalous groups. This has exacerbated tensions. In the presentations of petitions, for example, protocol has not been followed. In the Konkomba petition, one clause contained an open threat of violence.

Ethnic relations have, of course, varied from place to place, depending on the claims made. For example, one respondent described how, among the Konkomba at Saboba, land and political independence are claimed, and relations were particularly poor with the chiefly groups also claiming authority. On the other hand, in Bimbilla town there was a certain level of sharing and integration with the Nanumba and, in Dagbon, inter-marriage.

The importance of certain bellicose individuals in generating and orchestrating aggression and organising for war cannot be underestimated.

Communications and rumours of war

Tensions were further heightened because of rumours of war circulating in the press and by word of mouth. NGOs had started gathering data about rumours in the previous rainy season.[35]

The circulation of certain documents exacerbated tension, such as copies of the Konkomba demand for paramountcy. Inflammatory statements were also made in Parliament by MPs from the various groups. Circulation of rumours in the press increased tensions.

The sparks

At the end of January 1994, tensions greatly increased in the Nanumba District when police intercepted a shipment of arms heading for Bimbilla. This led to the destruction of the Bimbilla police station by a Nanumba mob, who seized arms, ammunition, and tear gas held there. A week later, a dispute over the price of a guinea fowl at Nakpayili market in the same District sparked off full-scale violence.

Conclusion

Cairns (1997) argues that risks of war are increased when the following conditions are satisfied:

- Societies are divided by ethnic or religious identity, particularly if people see that they suffer because of belonging to their group and they blame the other group for this.
- There is intense competition over the means to earn a living, particularly if the competition is rapidly increasing and the means are decreasing.
- There is no framework to permit peaceful change.

All these factors operated in northern Ghana.

As Pul argues,[36] ethnic groups are interdependent, and the conflict represents an attempt to redefine the terms of this interdependence, in the absence of any legitimate process to contain it. Chieftaincy and land issues are markers in this process of redefinition.

... the fact that the conflicts exist and persist in the region is an indicator of some degree of interdependence among the various parties to the conflict. The conflict situation represents attempts of the parties to redefine the terms of their independence; namely production relationships, power relationships, access to and control over productive resources etc. For instance, the issues frequently mentioned as the immediate causes of the conflict are those related to the subjects of chieftaincy and land. But it must be realised that no one is fighting for chieftaincy and land for their own sake. Beyond these issues are deeper questions of the resources and opportunities these factors provide for cultural, material and even spiritual development for the members of the various groups.

The outbreak of wars represents the lack of or inadequacies of existing conflict resolution procedures to peacefully manage the process of redefinition of terms of inter-dependence. Consequently, frustration with the existing process has tended to breed aggression among the parties; and without the necessary safety valves to stem the violent reactions to the frustration, war breaks out.[37]

Principal causes of the 1994–5 conflict are depicted in Figure 5.

Figure 5: Causes of the 1994–5 war in northern Ghana

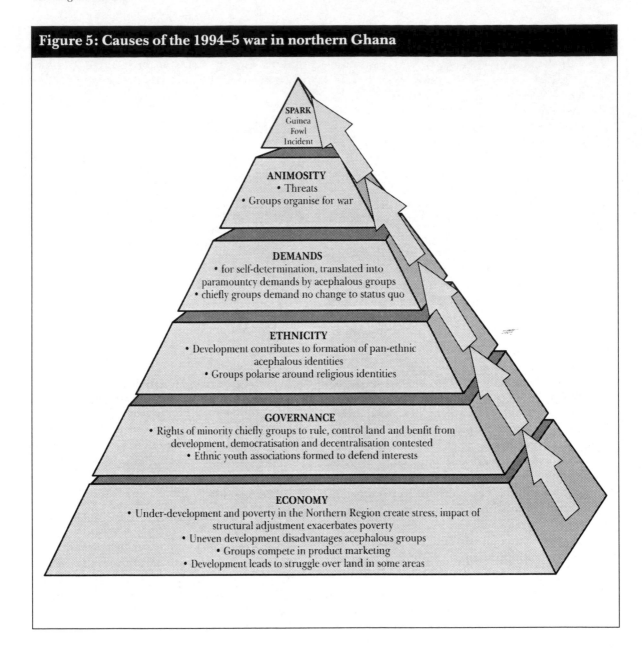

SPARK
Guinea
Fowl
Incident

ANIMOSITY
• Threats
• Groups organise for war

DEMANDS
• for self-determination, translated into
paramountcy demands by acephalous groups
• chiefly groups demand no change to status quo

ETHNICITY
• Development contributes to formation of pan-ethnic
acephalous identities
• Groups polarise around religious identities

GOVERNANCE
• Rights of minority chiefly groups to rule, control land and benfit from
development, democratisation and decentralisation contested
• Ethnic youth associations formed to defend interests

ECONOMY
• Under-development and poverty in the Northern Region create stress, impact of
structural adjustment exacerbates poverty
• Uneven development disadvantages acephalous groups
• Groups compete in product marketing
• Development leads to struggle over land in some areas

4 The war and its impact

The conflict

A dispute over the price of a guinea fowl between a Nanumba and a Konkomba at Nakpayili market near Bimbilla in Bimbilla District sparked off the conflict. It was described by a witness as follows.

A Nanumba and a Konkomba had a misunderstanding over a guinea fowl at the market. But they resolved the dispute in the market. The following day the Nanumba and his people went to farm. The Konkomba who lost the guinea fowl mowed down the buyer and his brothers. Three of them. So one escaped, ran to the house and gave the alarm. Before they could prepare, there was a counter charge from the same group of people. So they locked horns ...[38]

Within three days, fighting had spread into seven Districts. The first attack on Dagombas by Konkombas occurred at Nakpachei. The village was burned down. The fighting then spread north to the villages surrounding the Dagomba capital, Yendi. Except for Yendi and one nearby village, all Dagomba settlements in the District were burned down. The attacks met with little resistance, but a number of Konkomba settlements in the District were burned. Fighting also spread to the East Gonja District, where conflict was sparked off by a Nawuri killing of two Konkombas. Konkombas then allied with Nawuris to attack Gonjas.

The Districts affected were Nanumba, East Gonja, East Dagomba, Gushiegu-Karaga, Zabzugu-Tatale, Saboba-Chereponi and West Dagomba (see Figure 3). The principal areas of conflict were around Yendi, Salaga, Bimbilla, Gushiegu, Wulensi, Kpandai, Sekpiegu, and Zabzugu-Tatale. After 10 days of fighting, the government declared a state of emergency, and peace-keeping troops were sent in. The most intense fighting lasted for about one month. A major incident at the start of the conflict was a Gonja ambush of Konkombas at the strategic Buipe Bridge, a key point on the main Tamale–Kumasi road, where 20 people were killed. See Table 4 for a timeline for the conflict.

A combination of traditional and modern weaponry was used: AK47s, bows and poisoned arrows, and shotguns. Fighting techniques including surprise attacks, surrounding and burning villages, and gunning down fleeing populations. At the Dagomba village of Sambu, for example, the village was surrounded by 2,000 Konkombas and burned. Children were killed, and animals were slaughtered or taken.

Government response

The government response was delayed, because there was no means of communication between the Districts and central government. Reports by government officials, political leaders, and chiefs

Table 4: Conflict timeline

Year	Date	Events
1994	1 February	Konkombas attacked Nanumbas at Nakpayili, Nanumba District.
	2 February	Konkombas attacked Dagombas at Nakpachei, East Dagomba District. Nawuris attacked Konkombas at East Gonja District.
	10 February	State of emergency declared in 7 Districts, government peace-keeping troops arrive.
	February–March	Intense fighting in 7 Districts.
	June	Peace treaty signed.
1995	March	Nanumba–Konkomba violence at Bimbilla.

that were eventually transmitted to Regional authorities were not clearly acknowledged or quickly acted upon. However, after a meeting between the REGSEC and the Regional Minister, the peace-keeping troops were finally sent in.

The impact

Casualties and displacement

It is estimated that close to 15,000 people were killed during the conflict. The nature of the weaponry and fighting techniques used led also to widespread injuries. Psycho-social impacts have been severe, and human suffering untold. One interviewee described the case of a girl who lost both parents and five brothers. The Ghana Broadcasting Corporation televised an interview with a woman who described in detail the horrific killing of her baby son.[39]

By April 1994, it is estimated that 135,000 persons were displaced within the Region. By June 1995, the number stood at 160,000.[40] Others had been displaced to neighbouring Regions and even to Togo.[41] Bacho, Musah, and Mahama (1996:1) suggest a total figure for all displaced people of 200,000. As war raged, rural women and children of chiefly groups sought shelter in the District Capitals, notably Salaga, Bimbilla and Yendi. Others were taken to Tamale in government buses and private vehicles. Konkombas fled to Saboba, Wapilu, and Bimbonayili. Some displaced people relied on families to house, feed and shelter them. Training centres and other institutions were transformed into refugee camps for those without such connections.

While some groups returned to their villages very quickly after the fighting was over, other groups remained displaced for up to two years, and Tamale is still not accessible to Konkombas.

Impact on villages and households

At least 442 villages were destroyed.[42] In Bimbilla District, for example, 56 villages were burned down and ransacked in 1994. Of only eight villages not attacked at this time, three were targeted in March 1995 in a second round of attacks. This affected local coping mechanisms, as villages were torn apart and leaders killed.

The destruction and looting of family livestock and property, including agricultural implements, food and seeds, left many people destitute. One estimate of cattle losses in the

Nanumba District alone put them at 20,000.[43] After the conflict, a climate of insecurity prevailed: rates of theft of livestock and property remained high, and sporadic incidents, such as crop destruction, occurred.

Impact on agriculture

The impact on agriculture was severe. Since seed and agricultural implements had been destroyed, farmers found it difficult to restart production. As low-level conflict continued, including the sporadic destruction of crops, the climate of uncertainty dissuaded farmers from investing time and resources in production. Fears for security at the farm also affected cultivation. In Bimbilla, Yendi, and Salaga Districts, many displaced people farmed at their villages but could not stay there, for security reasons. Time spent travelling meant less time available for farming operations, and this affected yields. At Kpandai, Salaga, and Bimbilla, many farmers restricted their cultivation to the area around their compounds, since they were afraid to go to the bush to farm. Again, this affected yields.

The impact on agriculture affected food security in the area. A 1994 survey found that most food stocks in the targeted villages had been destroyed.[44] Many families faced by restrictions on farming were not able to meet even half of their food requirements. Food aid was provided for nine months (see below), but some farmers were not able to resume normal farming, even in the 1996–7 season.

At the same time, the agricultural extension and veterinary services were disrupted. This led to the spread of unchecked pests and disease. Owing to insecurity, the Agricultural Development Bank suspended loans. Three Farmers' Service Centres were destroyed and two looted in the conflict areas.[45]

Since this area is a major exporter of foodstuffs, lower yields affected food prices and national food stocks up to 1996. Cotton production in the conflict area has also been low, with adverse consequences for cotton companies.

Trade and marketing

The conflict also affected trade. In 1994 most market trade ceased for up to six months in the worst-affected areas. The huge markets of Nakpayili (livestock and yam) and Wulense (yam) ceased to function. Even after that, Konkombas found it difficult to stay at markets until the evening and they still do not go to Tamale market.

Impact on services and infrastructure

Education was halted in the conflict areas. In 1994, 65,384 children were displaced, 746 schools closed, and 2,500 teachers were affected. Schools were destroyed: 155 in total, including 24 in Salaga District alone. Others lost teachers and equipment. In 1997 many schools had still not reopened. One interviewee noted, 'This conflict has drawn education back by 10 to 15 years or even 50 years, the destruction that has been caused.'

Other service areas were disrupted as teachers, agricultural extensionists, health personnel, and other workers fled, and clinics, offices, and water sources were destroyed. The displacement of local Traditional Birth Attendants, smiths, and so on also had a severe impact.

NGO and other development work was affected. For example, GTZ (the German government development agency) withdrew its support to Nanumba District projects and later from Northern Region as a whole. Support from Christian Aid and Bread for the World for agricultural centres and literacy programmes in Saboba and Yendi is now in question.

The national economy has been affected by the allocation of vast government resources to its conflict-response programme.

Elections

The conflict also affected the timing, turnout, and voting patterns at the 1995 District Assembly elections in the areas directly affected by the fighting.

29

5 Peace-keeping and humanitarian relief and rehabilitation

Peace-keeping

The seven Districts under the State of Emergency were placed under a joint Military Task Force. There was a joint military–police presence in each of the District capitals, and detachments were sent to 12 villages where the tension was highest, to deter confrontation. The State of Emergency was lifted on 10 August 1994, one month later than expected, due to continuing insecurity. By then, peace-keeping activities were gradually being handed over to the police.

Despite the initial delay, the peace-keeping operation has been widely praised, by representatives of NGOs and civil society alike, as effective and judicious. This contrasts with government interventions in many other African conflicts.

The military were called in to separate warring groups and contain the conflict. There were some accusations that they occasionally compromised their neutrality during the conflict. However, most respondents paid tribute to the troops for halting the fighting, providing safety, aid, and medical services, and analysing situations in a measured way before acting.[46] One interviewee recalled, 'Soldiers picked up the wounded while it was unsafe to travel for NGOs.' Another said, 'The role of the police and army is appreciated, they didn't take accusations for granted.' An NGO official described the military group as 'peace-makers' and 'peace-brokers' who made sure they censured only the minority of warmongers.

Government relief and rehabilitation programmes

A timeline for relief and rehabilitation initiatives is given in Table 5. The government organised camps for the displaced, and the Task Force facilitated NGO relief distribution, providing escorts and sharing security information.

On 15 March 1994, the government appealed to the WFP for assistance. The response was prompt, and 11 tonnes of food aid was provided for a 150-day period. Assistance was later extended up to January 1995.

In June 1994, the Minister for Food and Agriculture made a needs-assessment. Consultation meetings were held with farmers throughout the conflict area.[47] Hoes and machetes were distributed during the tour. The government then implemented a relief package valued at 650 million cedis, containing hoes and power tillers. MoFA also provided tractor services, animal vaccinations, bull-lending for husbandry, stray-animal quarantine, training for bullock ploughing, seed multiplication, and pest control. The government also facilitated the return of agricultural officers. Finally, it negotiated for the Agricultural Development Bank to resume lending and soften its conditions for obtaining credit, and for the recommencement of agricultural inputs sales and services.[48]

The government also organised a rehabilitation programme to provide house-building materials. It was hampered in some areas by the continued tensions. For example, government attempts to resettle Gonjas near Kpandai failed, because of continued opposition between Gonjas and Nawuris.

The Ministries of Health and Education have also started to rehabilitate services with the co-operation of District Assemblies. The National Mobilisation Programme supported self-help initiatives and group projects, and funded agricultural and reconstruction ventures.

Funding was a major constraint on this relief programme. Government requests for donor funding met with little success. Most donors felt that relief channelled through NGOs would be more appropriate. This embarrassed the government and was a source of tension between NGOs and the government.

NGO relief and rehabilitation programmes

NGOs

NGOs in Northern Ghana have supported social development, agriculture, health, education, credit-provision, and well-digging for more than

Table 5: Government and NGO relief and rehabilitation efforts (NGO initiatives shaded)

Year	Date	Events
1994	February	Joint UN/NGO/government assessment mission.
		Start of local government relief.
		Start of individual NGO relief effort (Red Cross and Médicins sans Frontières).
	March	Government appeal to WFP. Food aid begins.
	April	Consortium relief initiative begins.
	May 5–19	NGO Consortium needs-assessment of all conflict areas.
	May	Needs-assessment complementary to Consortium assessment by Gubkatimali, Peronudas and Amasachina throughout conflict areas.
	May–June	Tours by government representatives, MoFA needs-assessment.
1995	January	WFP assistance ends.
	December	End of Consortium relief initiative.
1996	March	NGOs assist with reconciliatory rehabilitation projects.
	May–July	Consortium rehabilitation needs-assessment.

20 years. Programmes have become part of the essential social-services infrastructure, complementing government services or compensating for the lack of them. The aim of most NGOs is 'development'; in interviews they said it was necessary 'to abandon their development programmes for relief' during and after the conflict. This was inevitable, because of the NGOs' close relationships with various groups of the population.

The Inter-NGO Consortium

At first, individual NGOs provided relief in the conflict areas. The Inter-NGO Consortium began as an informal, co-operative response to the 1994 conflict. Although not operational itself, it attempted to co-ordinate NGO efforts. The Consortium drew up a relief programme. The international agencies that had good relations with the government and international donors became the lead agencies.

The most active local NGO[49] members of the Consortium are Amaschina, Assemblies of God Development and Relief Services (AGDRS), Business Advisory Development and Consultancy Centre (BADECC), Catholic Secretariat, Council of Churches and related organisations, Gubkatimali, Penorudas, and Ti Yum Taaba Development Association (TIDA). The active international NGO members are ActionAid, Action on Disability and Development (ADD), Catholic Relief Services (CRS), Lifeline Denmark, Oxfam UK and Ireland (now known as Oxfam GB), the Red Cross, and World Vision.

Needs-assessment

Defining their mandates as 'humanitarian aid', the NGOs started collecting and publishing information about the conflict. Two NGO assessment missions were undertaken in May 1994, aiming to provide an informed basis for the relief effort. Help was provided in line with these and with government assessments from April 1994. This was when the worst of the fighting was over, and NGOs could begin to access the war zones.

Donors

The principal multilateral and bilateral donors who supported this programme were UNICEF, the World Food Programme (WFP), and the ODA (UK Overseas Development Administration[50]). Others included the Red Cross, international churches, and the British High Commission. The Consortium made funding requests as a collective body, and the response was positive.

Camps for the displaced

Apart from the camps organised by the Districts, the NGOs and religious leaders organised camps in the District capitals. Access was possible with the co-operation of the Military Task force, who provided protective escorts. There were complaints that the army expected 'backhanders' from the aid, and inevitably some relief items found their way to the army; but most aid was delivered straight into the conflict area by NGOs and distributed to the needy. The Military Task Force also provided useful assistance in the form of updates on the security situation and guarding of the camps.

Relief aid and strategy

Food aid was funded by the WFP, and non-food aid (including food and blankets, sleeping mats, buckets and so on) by the German, Chinese, and Swiss Red Crosses and Oxfam. To ensure neutrality as well as efficiency, this aid was distributed by a group of NGOs, including the AGDRS, the Council of Churches, and other local NGOs. These were called 'joint neutral teams'. Even then, some NGO staff were accused of favouring members of their own ethnic groups. On the other hand, some NGO staff said they had to work 'under cover' to reach victims of ethnic groups other than their own, to avoid criticism from their own groups.

In the displaced-people's camps, the approach was to support the cohesion and coping strategies of families, and the existing gender-determined division of labour. Aid was principally channelled through male household heads, but was distributed to women where widows had become household heads. The Red Cross arranged for aid distribution to be supervised by a woman. NGOs organised sanitation work by mobilising volunteers and leaders from among the displaced.

The registration of aid recipients by NGO teams was led by AGDRS staff who had previous experience of working in conflict. The Red Cross, TIDA, and BADECC were also involved. WFP later insisted on a re-registration by the AGDRS. There were 152,600 refugees registered. Needs were then assessed and distribution mechanisms established. District co-ordinators were appointed to monitor distribution.

One problem was the difficulty of distinguishing displaced people from the local population, which necessitated lengthy investigations. Another problem was mollifying local people who complained that there was more aid for the displaced than for them. A further difficulty was how to communicate information about relief aid to all population groups. Konkombas staying in remote areas were not always informed, and this led to misunderstanding and fear about the relief effort among them. Some Konkombas were not included in the initial relief aid, although coverage was better after the second registration.

Agricultural relief

The NGOs also provided aid to assist refugees in restarting agriculture. Seeds were purchased and distributed under the umbrella of the NGO Consortium. This was funded by the ODA with ActionAid, CRS, Oxfam, and World Vision (these were also involved in distribution). A second distribution of seeds, recommended at the end of 1995 in the evaluation report of the first relief distribution, was never undertaken. This was due to lack of co-ordination among NGO Consortium members and to administrative delays. NGOs also provided fertiliser, cutlasses, and hoe blades.[51]

There was various other assistance, including gifts from the Danish Community Project, the Chinese Red Cross, and the Ghanaian Red Cross. A private company, Ghana Cotton Company Limited, also provided assistance. It ploughed 3,000 acres and provided food and cotton seeds for farmers in the Gushiegu area.[52]

The relief effort continued for a year and a half. As the Consortium established its procedures and working methods, its organisation improved.

Evaluation

UNICEF evaluated the NGO relief operation.[53] Its report found that the programme had many strengths, including the 'co-ordinated program; the pooling of resources and co-ordination of resource allocation' and the fact that 'Impartial identity for all NGOs was obtained'. This meant that 'The immediate food security issues of the displaced people were addressed immediately following the 1994 conflict.'

However, UNICEF noted that the Consortium was weak in its general lack of emergency preparedness, the absence of an institutional framework, and a failure to address the multi-sectoral character of needs in an integrated approach. Also, there were difficulties in the quality of aid delivery and supervision.

Inevitably, there were some problems linked to the problems of collaboration among organisations of different aims and interests, rationales, sizes, capacities, profiles, and connections. However, co-ordination was achieved, even though each NGO used its respective administrative systems while the Consortium was drawing up a common programme, budget, and funding requests.

Post-conflict NGO rehabilitation

NGOs carried out limited rehabilitation work up to 1996. Some NGOs initiated projects, such as new schools and clinics, implemented by groups consisting of members of previously warring groups. These acted as models to demonstrate the possibility of reconciliation and regeneration through shared work.

In 1996, the Consortium initiated a rehabilitation assessment that identified immediate resettlement and rehabilitation needs.[54] It was funded by Oxfam and UNICEF. The assessment report identified the groups who continued to be vulnerable as a result of the conflict and the organisation of relief efforts:

- **Disabled people:** Disablement as a result of the conflict made people entirely dependent on relatives. People who had been disabled before 1994 had often lost their occupations as a result of the conflict.
- **Children:** Under-fives' malnourishment rates in the conflict areas were as high as 60 per cent in 1996. There were large numbers of orphans, and of children who had not gone back to school.
- **Widows:** Widows, often with many children, had to find a source of livelihood and were not always capable of providing for the family. Aid was mainly targeted at male family heads, and so widows did not have access to basic materials. House-repair for widows was not included in the government rehabilitation programme. Food relief that had been targeted at women heads of households was discontinued, although it was still required in many cases.

- **Women in general:** In many cases, community-based organisational structures set up to support relief efforts did not include women. Women continued to need support in their productive and reproductive roles to revive their coping strategies, for the following reasons:
  - Women had lost working equipment and capital in the conflict, and since many villages lost grinding mills or other processing equipment, women were now grinding grain by hand, which prevented them from engaging in other activities.
  - Women's groups had disintegrated, resulting in a loss of this source of mutual support, and precluding access to rehabilitation aid for villages.
  - Women were particularly suffering from the decline in 'formal' antenatal provision (which resulted in a 50 per cent reduction in attendance rates). The services of Traditional Birth Attendants were also scarce, because many of them had also been displaced.

A rehabilitation funding request was formulated in mid-1997, following participatory research into food shortages in May 1997.

NGO/government co-operation

There was considerable co-operation between NGOs and government in the areas of camp organisation, military escorts, and information-sharing, as described. Meetings were held between the Military Task Force relief committee and the Consortium co-ordinator, although these tailed off over time. The Consortium even provided a vehicle for the government's rehabilitation programme. However, national-level collaboration was more problematic, because there was a degree of competition for donor funding, and NGOs were more successful in gaining it. Co-ordination of funding proposals was difficult. One interviewee said:

Delays in the preparation of joint funding proposals and the result, a lack of operational collaboration in execution, may have contributed to a degree of mistrust hindering NGO/government relations at national level.

6 The peace process

Government peace initiatives

Apart from its highly successful peace-keeping operations, the government also set up a Permanent Peace Negotiation Team (PPNT). Consisting largely of chiefs from other Regions and headed by a member of the Council of State, the PPNT made several missions to the various ethnic groups and held talks. It held meetings in Tamale, the conflict districts, and Accra and Kumasi with chiefs, opinion leaders, and the Northern Regional Security Committee. An arbitration approach was taken, with the PPNT acting as an intermediary. Four delegates from each of the warring factions were invited to present their cases to the PPNT. In June 1994 a Peace Treaty was signed with the warring factions. They agreed to lay down their arms and submit to the government security agencies. However, each faction signed separately, and the legitimacy of some signatories was in doubt. Therefore the process did not foster significant trust or the beginnings of reconciliation. Respondents also noted that the delayed government response to the conflict in February 1994 left deep suspicions among some local leaders that the government had acted in a partisan manner, rather than seeking a lasting and just settlement. They felt that the government was not now to be trusted to facilitate a fair peace.

The peace treaty had limited success. Fighting broke out again in March 1995.

The PPNT suffered from a lack of financial support and facilitation skills. In August 1995 it invited the NGO Consortium and the NPI to provide such skills. This invitation was not accepted, because the Consortium was afraid it might compromise its 'independent' position. Another problem was that the PPNT is remote from the northern context, with its head office in Accra, 400 miles from the nearest conflict zone.

PPNT meetings with individual ethnic group leaders resulted in two reconciliation ceremonies, at Yendi on 21 December 1995, and at Salaga on 18 May 1996. These took place after peace had been brokered by the Consortium between Dagombas and Konkombas and between Gonjas and Konkombas, Bassares, and Nchumurus. The President's attendance at each of these ceremonies lent them weight. They included sacrifices according to the customs of each ethnic group. However, the Konkombas did not attend the ceremony in the Gonja area, saying the notice given to them was too short. They later sent a delegation to make a formal apology to the President for this snub.

Table 6 presents the chronology of all the peace initiatives. It shows that PPNT successes, such as the peace ceremonies, built upon NGO-initiated peace work.

NGO initiatives

The reconciliation and peace process promoted by the NGO Consortium began in September 1994. The objective was to end violence in the short term and to promote sustainable peace in the long term, through changing perceptions, attitudes, and building new relationships among societies in the region. The rationale for the work was as follows:

... first that development projects undertaken by Non-Governmental Organisations in the region have stultified and secondly, that in the absence of real peace, there can be no meaningful development in the region nor would any tangible gains be realised from the democratic structures that have been put in place with decentralisation ... through the functioning of the District Assemblies. In the past year, development activities have been suspended while focus is on relief work to help displaced people in the Region. Since most of these organisations are not specialised in relief activities, an important consideration is given to the management of the conflict so that it will be possible to resume normal programmes ...[55]

NGOs recognised that the primary responsibility for the maintenance of peace rested with the government, so they aimed to complement the government's peace work. However, NGOs needed to act, because

Table 6: Timeline of peace initiatives in northern Ghana (NGO initiatives shaded)

Year	Date	Events
1994	April	PPNT created.
	June	Peace treaty signed. Tours by government representatives.
	September–November	PPNT field visits.
	November	NPI and Consortium initial consultation meeting, followed by a week's reconciliation needs-assessment in the conflict areas.
1995	April	Second NPI and Consortium reconciliation needs-assessment following renewal of conflict.
		Individual NGO follow-up field visits begin.
	May 16–18	Kumasi I peace workshop.
	May	PAC (follow-up committee) formed, peace programme began in all conflict areas.
	June 26–29	Kumasi II peace workshop.
	October	Peace seminar for chiefs at Damongo.
		Peace education in Zabzugu-Tatale and Nanumba Districts.
		Christian Council of Ghana organises seminars for peace and reconciliation for Christians in conflict areas.
	November	Peace education in West Dagomba District.
	December 16–19	Kumasi III peace workshop.
	December	PAC peace campaign in East Gonja and Saboba-Chereponi Districts.
		Peace seminar at Salaga with youth association, women's group representatives, opinion leaders, and representatives of security forces.
		PPNT-led peace ceremony at Yendi between Dagombas and Konkombas.
		Joint Islamic-Christian prayers for peace held at Yendi.
1996	January	Peace seminar at Tamale with youth association, women's group and opinion leaders, and representatives of security forces.
	February 26–9	Kumasi IV peace workshop, draft peace agreement drawn up. Local consultations on the agreement made in the Districts.
	March 27–30	Kumasi V peace workshop, peace agreement signed.
	May	PPNT-led peace ceremony at Salaga between Gonjas and Konkombas.
	July–September	Local Council of Churches' campaign to encourage formation of Christian and Muslim Working Committees.
	August	Consortium and youth association leaders meet to discuss creation of a pan-Regional youth association.
	October 11–13	Kumasi VI peace workshop, NORYDA created.

... the basis of sustainable development for which most NGOs exist cannot be attained when the efforts of the NGOs and the communities they work with are cyclically undermined by the destruction of human and material resources that accompany the outbreak of violence in the Region.[56]

The peace process consisted of a reconciliation needs-assessment followed by a peace-awareness campaign, involving a series of workshops with leaders of the warring factions held in Kumasi,[57] and grassroots-level work, which continued after the Kumasi series ended. The timeline of the process is given in Table 6. Funding and other support was provided by UNICEF, ODA, and NGOs.

Peace and Reconciliation Working Group

The Consortium created a Peace and Reconciliation Working Group (PRWG) consisting of six NGO staff to organise and evaluate the peace process with the Peace Awareness Committee (see below). The PRWG stipulated that the NGOs were there to facilitate and empower the people in the conflict area to work towards their own solutions. In other words, the approach was to facilitate conciliation rather than to arbitrate between the parties, as attempted by the PPNT. The Consortium's work was to support leaders who were accountable to their communities and to use consultative methods and process. Chiefs, acephalous leaders, and other community leaders were to play the main role, in order to increase their 'ownership' of the peace process. Transparency and momentum were to be promoted.

The Consortium also appointed a co-ordinator for the follow-up process, made available by BADECC, and provided logistical support. This permitted a series of visits to the different Districts to take place, undertaken by ASRDP, ActionAid, Amasachina, TIDA, and Penorudas. However, the co-ordinator met with an unfortunate accident, and the car was out of use from April 1996.

The Nairobi Peace Initiative

The Nairobi Peace Initiative (NPI, a Kenyan NGO) was invited to assist in the process. The NPI has experience in mediation and peace-making in many African civil conflicts, at both local and national levels. Training is undertaken in the form of reconciliation workshops and seminars. The director has published widely on conflict resolution and mediation in civil wars.

The NPI philosophy[58] considers peace to be the transformation of conflicting and destructive interactions into more co-operative and constructive relationships, where the inter-dependence of people is acknowledged. It is based on the following principles:

- There are spiritual, psychological, social, and ecological levels of existence. Reconciliation involves making peace with God, self, neighbours, and nature, and it demands the restructuring of relationships.[59]
- Conflict cannot be resolved unless the root causes are identified and dealt with.
- Conflict cannot be resolved unless there is a just and fair resolution process as well as outcome.
- The deep needs of people are not totally incompatible.

This holistic vision demands a holistic approach. The NPI aims to work out an in-depth understanding of peace for those in conflict resolution. Its goal is to find common ground among people in conflict and to facilitate consensus-building. It then seeks to enhance community values, which the NPI regards as more significant in the African context than individualism.[60]

Key problems and opportunities

The task of developing strategies was challenging, because of the complexity of the situation and the multiplicity of actors and power brokers, including politicians, traditional leaders, youth associations, Christian and Islamic organisations, the army and police, the PPNT, the Regional Administration and District and Regional Security Councils, local and international NGOs, and citizens.

It was also problematic because some NGOs and churches had close links with certain groups because of their work or personnel. This created an impression that they were partisan, putting their neutrality in question. A further problem was that, as the December 1996 elections approached, some aspiring politicians saw advantages in undermining government peace efforts.[61]

Peace-awareness campaign

The campaign was planned at three levels: community, Regional, and national. A Peace Awareness Committee (PAC) was formed to take up the planning and implementation of the peace campaign at the first Kumasi workshop (see below). It consisted of eight members from the four warring factions. The PAC was created as a civil-society organisation, with the aim of leading the peace process, calling on the assistance of the Consortium and NPI as required. Funds for the peace programme were to be raised on behalf of the PAC.

Grassroots work

In preparation for the Kumasi workshops
The NPI and individual NGOs worked with chiefs and community leaders at the grassroots level to bring about peace. The process started at the community level, identifying possible peacemakers and ways in which peace might be brought about in this context.

In April 1995, the NPI together with the NGOs undertook a working visit to all the conflict areas. The main purpose was to be properly informed and educated and to ... listen to all the parties involved in the conflict, the victims, community activists, chiefs and elders and Regional and District political leaders. It was also ... [a] unique opportunity to begin to identify 'voices of reason' in all the conflict areas. The best peacemakers would have to come from the communities at conflict. [They would be] ... people who through their influence appealed for non-violence and even assisted in saving the lives of some of their adversaries. Such people were the bridge-builders who were identified and through their engagement would later engage others. Such an expanding engagement it was envisaged would gradually permeate the different communities and thereby facilitate peace building designs.[62]

The NPI and Consortium met a cross-section of the population and Regional and District authorities. There were also special meetings with community activists and opinion leaders. These interactions gave a wide perspective on the conflict and causes of the conflict that would have to be addressed. The need for an intervention was apparent: people called for more peace work by the government.

The outcome of these meetings was that the team was able to establish the goodwill and the confidence of political and community leaders. This was demonstrated in the enthusiastic reception and willingness to talk openly about the conflict throughout the affected areas.[63]

The NPI then designed an immediate follow-up programme. Selected NGO staff returned to the conflict areas and met the 'voices of reason' who had been identified earlier on, on a one-to-one basis.[64] These were then invited to participate in a series of peace workshops.

During and after the Kumasi workshops
Local peace education subsequently took the following form:

Leaders from the four ethnic communities [moved] from one community to another, talking to people and engaging them to accept the values of peace. In this effort they are assisted by the NGOs in the basic minimum logistics, such as transportation and other needs, while the presence of NPI enables a continuous search for alternatives ... ensuring a careful implementation of the peace initiatives. A periodic assessment of the extent of the impact of these campaigns helps to re-focus strategy as ... required.[65]

The flexibility of the approach is evident here.

October 1995 to February 1996 saw a programme of field meetings, leading up to the signing of the Kumasi peace agreement. Field visits were made in East Gonja, Saboba-Chereponi, Gushiegu-Karaga, Nanumba, East and West Dagomba Districts. They involved peace-education messages and campaigning in local languages by leaders of ethnic groups working in the areas of former 'opposing' ethnic groups, using the dove as a widely recognised peace symbol. Discussions took place with a broad cross-section of the community. However, financial constraints prevented extended work.[66]

Regional level
The strategy at the Regional level was as follows:

... to engage more actors to become peace builders ... Another aspect of peacemaking at this level is engaging chiefs, and by regular contacts continuing to reassure them of the absolute need for peace in order for development work to proceed smoothly in their communities. From this point of view, the chiefs consistently have to be beseeched to appeal to their people not to fight again when provoked.[67]

Peace seminars were held in East Gonja, Saboba-Chereponi, Gushiegu-Karaga, Nanumba, East and West Dagomba Districts, aimed at a wider constituency of youth-association leaders, women's representatives and opinion leaders, local NGO staff, District authorities, Divisional chiefs, and security-force representatives. These were facilitated by the NPI.

The process was boosted by the momentum begun at the first Kumasi workshop.

Work at the national level

At the national level, attention was focused on 'supporting the PPNT to enhance their capacity in completing the work of negotiations among the leadership of the four ethnic groups and dealing with the outstanding issues of the conflict'[68] through the second and subsequent Kumasi workshops. This was less successful than the local and Regional-level work.

The process encountered management problems and co-ordination problems because of the practical difficulties of getting the PRWG, PAC, and other actors together and ensuring their commitment in the face of the other work that members were engaged in.[69]

Kumasi Peace Workshops

The basic principle behind the workshops was that the warring groups should be assisted to consult among themselves to resolve their differences.

Kumasi I

The workshop was organised by the Consortium and NPI, and funded by ActionAid and AGDRS. It was attended by representatives of the NPI and the Consortium and leaders of the four warring factions, invited on the basis of the roles they played as 'voices of reason' during and after the conflict and on the basis of their individual capacities, their influence in the communities, and the respect they commanded. Importance was attached to the fact that the individuals did not represent any groups that were party to, or had an interest in, the conflict. When issuing invitations, the Consortium was careful to try to avoid raising expectations in the communities.

This was the first time since the conflict that all the parties had sat together in one room. The organisation and the contents of the workshop therefore had to be packaged very sensitively. The basis on which the invitations were issued was a 'consultation on resettlement and development in the conflict areas of the Northern Region'.

The overt aim of this initial workshop, then, was to ask how NGOs could continue development work in the Region, but the long-term goal was to enable the participants to see the possibilities for peace-making in their communities. The workshop followed the principle that communities must be able to see themselves as the best people to solve their own conflict, while the Consortium 'shared their pain', 'encouraged', and 'facilitated' the return to peace.[70]

The workshop began with a confidence-building exercise that promoted group dynamics. The workshop then looked at the issue of conflict in Africa and in northern Ghana in particular. The concept of mediation was discussed and distinguished from arbitration, and the NPI's peace paradigm was introduced. Participants were challenged to apply these values and become peace-makers. Participants asked for forgiveness from each other, agreed to stop making accusations, and hoped that this position would build confidence among people in the region and convince them that peace was possible. The damage and causes of the war were then discussed and what needed to be done. This led to the expression of further regret and remorse and increased the sense of urgency to begin building peace. Participants then looked at what they would do to further peace, and what was expected of the NPI and the Consortium. Participants were invited to consider what role they could play in counselling their own people to accept peace work.[71]

These first consultations were confidential, to protect the process from external pressures at that stage. The following needs emerged from the workshop:[72]

- To organise meetings by participants to educate people on the effects of the war.
- To form teams of people from different ethnic groups to preach peace throughout the conflict areas.
- To contact chiefs, MPs, opinion leaders, and youth leaders to promote free movement in the conflict areas and to organise a similar workshop for them.
- For NPI and the Consortium to assist the PPNT.
- For more dialogue between the paramount chiefs and the NPI/Consortium.
- For the Consortium to provide logistical support for peace work.

There was a response to most of these needs, with the exception of support for the PPNT. The PAC was set up to organise peace work. They later requested the Consortium to organise Kumasi II.

Kumasi II

As agreed at Kumasi I, the second workshop was widened to incorporate those who could influence events towards peace because of the positions they held. Participants were drawn from the following groups:

- Four or five leaders from each of the ethnic groups.[73] These included two MPs, six DCEs, two PPNT members, six chiefs (Nanumba, Konkomba, Gonja and Dagomba), and 12 youth association leaders and other opinion leaders.
- Two NPI staff.
- Seven representatives of the Consortium from ActionAid, AGDRS, the Council of Churches, CRS, Oxfam, World Vision, and BADECC.

Widening of participation was possible because Kumasi II had built on the work with communities:[74]

... maintaining the trust that had been built had to be taken into account by developing a mechanism that will allow continuous interaction, visits and exchange of views. Such activities facilitated the possibility for this second workshop, which was larger and more delicate because of the political dimension manifested by the presence of all the political heads of the Districts affected by the conflict.

The objectives, agenda, and ground rules for the Kumasi II workshop are presented as an example in Appendix 1.

The workshop considered NPI and the Consortium as 'partners' in the peace process.[75] The discussion was contextualised by considering the incidence and cause of conflict in Africa in general. A definition of conflict was agreed as follows: 'incompatible behaviour between parties whose goals *are* or *appear to be* incompatible or clashing'. The extent of the damage was then discussed. Participants were next divided into groups according to ethnicity, and the reasons for the conflict were discussed.

The workshop report[76] observes the progress at this stage.

... all participants felt a great sense of frankness had been demonstrated by all the groups and this initiated the collective reconciliation process within this group... There was a common sense that the communication gap that had existed all along was now being bridged ... There was the beginning of the expression of 'we were all wrong and none of us gained anything from this senseless war'. [There] was the eagerness to move forward and do something together to ameliorate the situation and work towards a sustainable peace.

The workshop then looked at ways of moving forward in single ethnic-group discussions. To plan more concretely, participants then divided into role groups (MPs, chiefs, DCEs, opinion leaders, youth leaders, and the PPNT). Positive and workable plans were the outcome.

The workshop was evaluated according to a written questionnaire. A sample of responses shows the success of the workshop:[77]

From the lesson of Peace and Reconciliation Philosophy, I have learned that reconciliation is possible when differences are openly discussed ... For the first time since the last war, I have spoken openly and freely to my opponents without the presence of any security personnel.

I learned to tolerate and accommodate the views of people other than my ethnic affiliation, and saw the people from the other side of the conflict are equally prepared for conflict resolution; I had been thinking that it was only my side. If the approach to these meetings continues, we can see peace in sight ... More grease to NPI. After all, the government mediation committee has failed the nation in resolving this conflict.

The main purpose of Kumasi I and II was to generate peace. The peace achievements that went in tandem with these workshops are listed in Appendix 2.

The NPI's holistic approach was vital to the facilitation of the peace process. By bringing together leaders involved in the conflict in person, space was provided for all points of view to be expressed, challenged, and reassessed. The process was difficult, because fear, mistrust, and hatred had to be overcome. The NPI urged participants 'to stop pointing fingers and to admit the mistakes that were made while reaching out to the other side in the hope that the conflict can now take a positive turn towards resolution through reconciliation'.[78] Eventually, participants on all sides began to express contrition, and participants began to desire peace and development more than conflict. One report described this process as follows:

The sense of remorse and regret among the participants further increased when together they assessed the damages brought about by the conflict. Together they shared the sad reality of their communities becoming dependent on relief aid when the region used to be the bread basket of the country. The long litany of destruction and damages was revealing enough. No one could express the sense of urgency to bring peace to the region more than the participants themselves.[79]

It was evident that at Kumasi II positions were not completely polarised and that a way forward was possible. From then on, participants took an active role in promoting peace, by sharing the process and results of the workshops in their communities of origin, and in formerly opposed communities.

Kumasi III

At Kumasi III, the workshop was opened to wider community participation, although the content was similar to that of Kumasi II (see Appendix 1). For the first time, women community leaders were included in the discussions. These leaders continued to participate in subsequent workshops.

The representatives of the ethnic groups expressed their grievances about the situation, described the damages and loss suffered due to the conflict, and again gave their views about the causes of the conflict. The way forward was then discussed (see Appendix 4 for details). It called for:

- A discussion of the PPNT's role.
- Debate to be held at a future workshop on the role of the chiefs in creating paramountcies and making reforms.
- The creation of a new pan-Regional youth association for the promotion of peace, security, arms control, and rumour control, with Regional and local consultative committees. A planning committee was to be set up and possible members identified.
- Rehabilitation and reconciliation.
- A continuing follow-up field programme.

Progress after the first three workshops

At the end of these three workshops it was evident that the process had moved forward.[80]

- There was a general willingness among Dagombas for a dialogue with Konkombas on the issues of land, traditional councils, and paramountcy.
- The Konkombas also showed a willingness to talk. They said they wanted recognition of their chiefs in the Nanumba District, and not land.
- The Nanumbas were moved to say that they would consider appointing Konkomba elders.
- Gonjas said that they were prepared to live peacefully with Konkombas.

Positions had come even closer together, and there were positive indicators that the problems could be resolved.

Kumasi IV

At the fourth Kumasi meeting, there were 48 delegates from seven ethnic groups consisting of chiefs, PPNT delegates, opinion leaders, and youth leaders. They worked towards a durable resolution to the conflicts. The NPI facilitated bilateral and multilateral negotiations to identify the issues and find solutions acceptable to all parties involved. The delegates severally and jointly agreed to a draft document outlining the agreements reached on the contentious issues brought up in the negotiations. The delegates then took away the draft agreement, for extensive consultation with all segments of their communities.

Kumasi V and the Peace Accord

After four weeks, the delegates returned to Kumasi for the fifth workshop, to report on the outcome of the consultation process. The amendments generated by the consultations were incorporated into the agreement. Some sections required re-negotiation in the light of consultation feedback. Delegates signed the Kumasi Accord on Peace and Reconciliation Between The Various Ethnic Groups In The Northern Region of Ghana on 30 March 1996 (see Appendix 5). This symbolised a commitment by all to find a proactive solution to all the problems that breed conflict in the Region. The Accord was widely reported in the press.

Kumasi VI and NORYDA

Ethnic groups participating in the Kumasi workshops wished to set up a forum for continued dialogue to assist in the prevention of future conflict, and this was called for in the Accord. The forum was conceived as the Northern Region Youth and Development Association (NORYDA) at a meeting facilitated by the Consortium in August 1996 with leaders from each of the youth associations. It was formally constituted at Kumasi VI as a broad body with representatives from all ethnic youth associations in the Northern Region. An interim executive committee was formed. NORYDA's first constitution was ratified on 13 October 1996. Widespread agreement and support was shown in the appended signatures of 31 chiefs and youth-association leaders representing 12 ethnic groups. Plans were put in place to set up an office in Tamale.

The creation of NORYDA is highly significant. As a widely representative organisation of ethnic groups in the Region, it constitutes the potential for a fundamental shift in Regional politics and a basis for sustainable peace. Developments in NORYDA are discussed below.

The workshop also reviewed the Accord to identify obstacles in it which mitigated against peace. The Gonja/Nawuri problem was revisited, and continuing differences were discussed.[81] Both parties agreed to consult their home communities and to find ways to bring about peace. The Gonjas said they were prepared to talk to the Gonja paramount about supporting the Nawuri desire for paramountcy.

The Kumasi Peace Agreement: issues addressed[82]

The Peace Accord is a series of separate agreements between different delegations. However, general issues can be identified.

Tension and belligerence

• The Accord commits the signatories to creating an enabling atmosphere of peace through forgiveness, moderation, compromise, and co-operation, in order to foster social reintegration and development.

• The arms build-up is condemned, and a commitment is made to stem the inflow of arms.

• The parties resolve to cease provocative acts and inflammatory statements in the media and to facilitate the free movement of people.

Land issues

• The Accord states that the allodial title, or ultimate ownership of land, is held only by existing paramount chiefs. Through this title, land is held in trust for all citizens of the respective areas, regardless of ethnic group.

• The Dagombas, Konkombas, and Bassares agree that divisional chiefs, whatever their ethnic group, are the caretakers of the land, and all citizens have an equal and unimpeded access to land in accordance with customary law.

Among the sixteen ethnic groups of the Northern Region, there seems to be no problem beyond resolution related to land tenure systems. The procedures for the acquisition of land for agricultural purposes seem to apply to all tribes and even people who come from other Regions to invest in agricultural activities.[83]

Chieftaincy and paramountcy issues

• The legitimate status of the paramountcies of the traditionally chiefly groups was confirmed.

• The legitimacy of the allegiance and associated customs demanded and paid to the traditional paramount chiefs of the ruling groups is confirmed.

• The legitimacy of chiefs among acephalous groups to be enskinned by the Paramount chiefs of different ruling ethnic groups is confirmed. The agreement foresees creation of such chief-ships in the near future.

• Both Konkombas and Bassares are to receive an unspecified number of paramountcies.

• The question of the 365 Konkomba self-appointed chiefs in Nanumba District will be looked into.

• The Nchumuru Paramountcy request will be supported by the Gonja Paramount chief in the National House of Chiefs.

Religious issues

• Mutual respect and sensitivity towards the religious practices of the different ethnic groups is to be shown.

• It was confirmed that the Nanumba earth priests should perform the land rituals in Nanun.

Discussion

Relationships between the ruling groups and the acephalous groups were calmed by the acceptance of the principle that all groups are entitled to paramountcy and other rights. This signifies a recognition of the rights and status of all ethnic groups by all parties.

The limited success of governmental initiatives had left a gap which the civil-society process filled. One interviewee, commenting on the Nchumuru paramountcy request, noted the effectiveness of the conciliation approach of the Kumasi workshops in this context: 'The PPNT honestly did not broker any peace between Gonja and Nchumurus ... it was Gonjas and Nchumurus who brokered peace, at Kumasi IV.'

The Kumasi Peace Agreement: outstanding issues

Even though older cephalous leaders have referred to versions of history which legitimise the status quo, at the end of the Kumasi peace process they were ready to compromise in most cases. However, the degree of compromise was sometimes regarded as insufficient by acephalous groups, such as the Nawuris and Nchumurus.

The most important unresolved issue is that of the Nawuri–Gonja conflict. It concerns the return to Kpandai of Gonja inhabitants, which the Nawuris oppose, and the resettlement of Nawuris in Kpembe and Salaga. Nawuris still claim land ownership over Kpandai, a claim still disputed by the Gonja. Nawuris still demand a paramountcy and request the Gonja paramount to grant it. Peaceful co-existence remains at stake here.

Peace projects initiated by NGOs and religious bodies

Several NGOs, including ActionAid, CRS, the Council of Churches, Islamic organisations, and ADD, initiated reconciliation projects with communities, resuming development work, but with a new focus. These NGOs also developed agendas for peace. This has had a positive influence on the peace process. Since October 1995, these individual programmes have gained momentum and are situated in all conflict-affected area Districts (though not every NGO works in every District). Examples are given here.

CRS and the Catholic Church

CRS and the dioceses have development and education programmes in all Northern Region Districts. Peace-education programmes were initiated in those communities which had been part of the conflict, including at Yendi, Tamale, and Damongo.

ActionAid

As part of its schools programme, ActionAid supported the rebuilding of schools. A notable example has been the Sunsun project in Saboba-Chereponi District. This involved the co-operation of the Konkomba and Dagomba communities, and children of both communities now attend this school.[84] The project has become a symbol of reconciliation. As a result of the project and through ActionAid peace education, 'the community in Chereponi and the surrounding Konkomba villages have started peace talks which have now filtered to other areas'.[85]

... communities have put in place checks and balances to deal with any potential threat to peace in the area. As a result of their good work, the [military] Task Force does not frequent the area, as the people ensure that peace prevails and any acts of aggression are dealt with decisively and quickly through the local system.[86]

... as a result of discussions ... the 33 disaster management committees, an apex body of both Konkomba and Anufo[87] *Wofo ('Peace') Committees, are setting up the Saware ('Peace') Committee. The Saware Committee will be recognised by the District Administration which has also been lobbied to create a Peace Committee reporting to the Regional Co-ordinating Council.*[88] *The Committee's function is to play a proactive role in conflict prevention strictly adhering to the traditional mode of conduct where all interested parties are consulted.*[89]

ActionAid sponsored a Wofo initiative in the Chereponi area whereby over 3,000 displaced people were absorbed back into their communities through the assistance of Wofo Committees.[90] ActionAid is also supporting a peace education campaign in two Junior Secondary Schools in every District affected by the conflict.[91]

Local Council of Churches

The Local Council of Churches has made an active contribution to the peace process. As an extension of its social development, a number of peace seminars and related events were organised, on themes including reconciliation, the role of the church in the democratic process, and women in the conflict. A peace programme was drawn up, with the following components:

- A schedule of peace and reconciliation work within churches in the conflict areas.
- A schedule to promote dialogue and co-operation among churches of all denominations and between Christians and Muslims.
- A commitment to play a central role in the peace efforts of the Consortium.

The Council has co-operated in organising dialogue between Muslim and Christian youth organisations, and joint prayer meetings with Christian and Muslim communities. A week of joint Christian and Muslim prayer meetings was held in December 1995 at Yendi. This eased tensions. The Ya-Na, the Dagomba paramount chief, had written a letter to the Archbishop forbidding a Catholic priest to work in Yendi. Because of reconciliation work, the Ya-Na later apologised and invited the priest to return.

Because of the links made between religious organisations and the causes of the conflict, there has also been a debate in the Christian church about the relationship between church development work and politics, and workshops were organised to clarify this.

The Council has also assisted in training teachers for the former conflict areas, incorporating courses in trauma counselling.

Amasachina

Amasachina is working with Dagomba and Konkomba communities on a joint project to build nurses' quarters at Kpatinga. This work is supported by the District Assembly and UNICEF.[92]

Relationship with the government

Government approval for NGO peace work

Consortium and NPI representatives met the Minister of Employment and Social Welfare, responsible for NGO affairs, and the Minister of the Interior in November 1994. The Minister for Employment and Social Welfare said that the government valued the NGO relief efforts and contribution to peace in the region. He welcomed the NGO desire to get involved in the peace process, saying it would be 'another feather' in the cap of NGOs. He urged the NGOs to incorporate civic education into their programmes and to develop peace messages for dissemination as part of community-level activities.[93] The Minister of the Interior made similar statements. Relations looked good, and NGO peace initiatives seemed to be welcomed. However, the NPI failed in attempts to meet the Minister of Defence and the PPNT Chairman. Relations with the PPNT later improved when PPNT members participated in several Kumasi workshops.

Relations between NGOs and District and Regional authorities

The first part of the NGO/NPI peace process saw good relations at this level.

The relations with political, Regional and District authorities were very open, co-operative and helpful during the first tour of NGO representatives with NPI of the conflict areas.[94]

District and Regional authorities wished to participate in the NGO conflict-resolution process, feeling that they had done all they could.

Some of these leaders admitted that they did not know how to handle the situation of senseless hostility and this explains the need for their involvement in the peace process.[95]

The Regional Minister was supportive of DCE involvement in the peace process and encouraged DCEs to attend Kumasi II. However, there were also elements of rivalry between the Consortium and the Regional administration, when the administration also made a proposal for funding for similar peace work.

Deterioration of relations

Relations between the government and the Consortium/NPI were later strained. The government did not accept the Kumasi peace agreement of March 1996. The delegation of chiefs, NGO representatives, and ethnic opinion leaders presenting the agreement to the government in Accra in May 1996 was not received, which was perceived as a significant snub. Interviewees gave several reasons for this. They said that the government played a significant role in West African peace initiatives, such as in Liberia, and was embarrassed that an NGO was required to negotiate peace within its own territory. Further embarrassment results from the fact that the NPI is a Kenyan NGO. Kenya does not have a good domestic peace record. Thirdly, the government felt that the PPNT had suffered from a lack of donor support, because NGOs had been in competition for this money.

Assessment of the situation and future prospects

Tensions began to subside in the conflict areas. By October 1995, for example, reports about the situation in Yendi stated: 'Dagombas and Konkombas have been moving along without any fear and they do brisk business.' In Saboba too, the situation was becoming calmer: 'During visits to Saboba, many Dagomba were also noted there in town, transacting business, and some of them said "it is now time to build a new united Region". [...] Dagomba and Konkomba Christians meet and worship together.'

However, in Tamale in 1996, Konkombas still did not have access. One interviewee said, 'Because, when we talk of free movement, the free movement is ... [everywhere except] in regards to Tamale. But of late I don't think it is as difficult as it was. Because Konkombas pass through ... but maybe we don't stop. Because of threats.'

The PRWG assessment

In January 1996 the PRWG assessed the peace-awareness campaign and the emerging peace. Findings included the following:
* The normal work schedules of members of the follow-up team interfered with peace-process activities and visits.

43

- Throughout the conflict area, communities' wounds were not yet healed. Certain areas were still considered 'no go'.
- The need for Konkombas to apologise to the Gonja paramount was still an issue.
- Certain attitudes still caused problems. For example, some Konkombas drove Nanumbas away from farming and enskinned their own chiefs in the Nanumba District.
- The dissemination of information by the PAC to the communities remained poor.
- People were inconsistent in what they said inside and outside meetings.
- There was a lack of trust among the activists in the PAC.
- Most of all, it was felt important that PAC should keep its focus and limit its relations with outside donors or partners other than the NPI, to maintain its strategic direction and thinking, withstanding the temptation of tied money offered. It was also acknowledged that peace is a slow process.

The situation in October 1998

The general situation is calm. Scaled-down government peace-keeping efforts contribute to this. The government has made it clear that violence will not be tolerated, and it will clamp down on any infringement. Rural–rural migration continues, as people move to areas where their ethnic groups predominate. Yendi is peaceful, and Konkombas are able to move there freely. Tamale is calm, but Konkombas still cannot enter the city. But Tamale is becoming ungovernable, owing to tensions between youth gangs (not related to ethnic issues).

Reconstruction proceeds, and in many places it is being carried out co-operatively among Konkombas, Dagombas, and Nanumbas. As well as the NGO work described, other agencies continue to support these schemes. The Canada Fund, for example, has supported the reconstruction of the Nakpayili market[96] (where the fighting first broke out). Agriculture has been re-started. It is evident that few village people will wish to fight again. The picture is generally positive.

The creation of the new paramountcies agreed under the Kumasi Accord is scheduled to go before the National and Northern Houses of Chiefs. However, although the Kumasi Peace Agreement provided for the enskinment of one Konkomba paramount, the Dagombas have decided to grant three paramountcies to Konkombas. The Konkombas had requested that only the divisional Chief of Saboba be raised to paramount status. They fear that they may become fragmented if three paramounts are created, because the paramounts may compete among themselves for followers. Konkombas regard this as a divide-and-rule tactic on the part of Dagombas. The Konkombas formally refused the offer of three paramountcies in April 1996. This could be a source of further conflict.

During the 1997–8 season there has been a food crisis in northern Ghana. Although centred on the Upper East Region, it has affected the Northern Region to some extent, and food aid has been supplied. This provides the setting for increased tensions, particularly in the Salaga area. Nawuris living at Kpandai claim that the District Assembly, dominated by Gonjas, has denied them food aid just as they have been denied other services. The District Assembly claims that Nawuris have refused the food aid (because they do not wish to draw on District services, which would indicate dependency rather than sovereignty over the Kpandai area). Another development in the Gonja–Nawuri crisis is that Gonjas have been trying to persuade the REGSEC to assist Gonjas to return to live in Kpandai.

The next stage of the democratisation process in Ghana is being implemented with the election of Unit Committees at sub-District level. The impact of this is yet to be felt.

The PPNT continues its work. The PPNT organises *ad hoc* village meetings in Accra and villages. Some of this work has a negative impact, because the PPNT is not always impartial. The PPNT currently has a poor relationship with Dagomba representatives, but a good relationship with Konkomba representatives.

The PRWG and PAC have been wound up, because they regarded long-term support for NORYDA, the new civil-society organisation, as the best way forward. The Consortium has taken a secondary role in the on-going peace process, acting as adviser and collaborator with NORYDA, and assisting NORYDA in obtaining funding. There is continued limited NPI involvement. NPI recently funded and facilitated a workshop on the role of the media in bringing peace, in collaboration with NORYDA.

New role for the Consortium

Although the Consortium is now less closely involved in the peace process, it is still active. In the face of the current food crisis, the Consortium has worked for seven months to put together a proposal for joint action and to lobby for funding to tackle the problem. This was initiated by Oxfam and ActionAid and carried out in conjunction with the Upper East regional government. It has involved carrying out a Rapid Rural Appraisal of the situation in the area. Unfortunately, donors have not been sympathetic to the NGOs so far, and the situation has been complicated by the fact that the central government put in a proposal for a relief programme at the same time.

Future prospects and NORYDA

Challenges

NORYDA faces several challenges. These include the unresolved tensions and new conflicts that have arisen in the Region since the Peace Accord:

- The continuing dispute between Nawuri and Gonja groups, which has been aggravated by the issue of food aid.[97] Nawuris continue to refuse to pay basic rates to the East Gonja District Assembly and to demand a separate District.
- Rival youth gangs in Tamale[98] threaten disturbance and new conflict.
- The new Dagomba–Konkomba dispute about numbers of paramountcies to be created.

Challenges also include continuing the peace campaign and attempting to get recognition for NORYDA by the grassroots communities, the government, and donors. An agenda has been set to continue meeting all opinion leaders, community leaders and chiefs, as well as NGOs and political and administrative authorities throughout the Region, in order to push forward the peace campaign and to gain recognition for NORYDA's work and status. NORYDA is experiencing financial problems and time constraints and has appealed for funding to organise a secretariat. At present, all NORYDA members are in employment elsewhere and so cannot commit much time to the project.

Finally, NORYDA faces the challenge of creating itself as a representative organisation in a hostile environment. Constituent youth associations can work together to foster peace. However, it is not clear whether they all have this intention. Smaller groups within NORYDA seem to be serious about peace, but the sincerity of some of the representatives of larger groups is questionable. NORYDA has been misrepresented to local communities by some of these leaders. A few of these NORYDA members do not actually represent their own youth associations, because the associations are factionalised. NORYDA faces derailment if individual representatives and constituent youth associations pursue their own personal or political interests at the expense of those of the wider group. Prominent and partisan press criticism of the representativeness of NORYDA also undermines its status in the Region.[99]

Achievements

NORYDA has achieved much so far. Despite the problems, it is developing itself as a representative, co-ordinated organisation with clear aims and objectives.

- Members have worked together on many issues. As this has gone on, good working relationships have been built up, and effective working practices established.
- NORYDA is a dynamic movement with a clear agenda for the future. As well as wishing to continue peace work and organise a secretariat, NORYDA aims to work and lobby for the development of the Region as a whole.
- NORYDA has received Oxfam funding for two years. This has allowed for the development of its capacities and the peace programme.

NORYDA is also working towards peace in innovative ways.

- It has worked with the NPI on a workshop about the role of the media in peace-making, as noted. Again, this addresses one of the causes of the 1994–5 conflict.
- NORYDA now co-ordinates the peace campaign. Innovative work has included organising broadcasts for peace on the new[100] Regional FM station, Savannah, incorporating discussions with paramount chiefs.

Finally, NORYDA has made a vital contribution towards settling disputes in several contexts.

- On the Kpandai issue, Oxfam and Consortium representatives have agreed to go with NORYDA to Kpandai and assess the situation.

- On the issue of social unrest in Tamale among rival youth gangs called the 'Uganda' and 'Rwanda Boys', NORYDA has worked to alleviate the tension.
- NORYDA has also worked to reduce conflict in the Mamprusi area (in a dispute between traditional authorities and the District Assembly over the siting of District offices).

- It has contributed to the resolution of a dispute in the West of the Region in the Mo area.
- It is working towards achieving free movement for all in Tamale, including Konkombas.

NORYDA has the potential to catalyse peaceful participatory social transformation and to work for equitable development for a sustainable peace and a better future.

7   Conclusion

The Consortium has played an important role in promoting the peace process among warring groups in northern Ghana. One very significant result was the facilitation of a participatory process leading to the Kumasi Peace Accord, which tackles some of the major causes of conflict, and a follow-up process that led to the creation of NORYDA. The process was a challenging one. Problems were encountered on the way, and difficulties remain. These include certain unresolved ethnic tensions and problems of co-operation with the government. However, the process is instructive and is an example of best practice in conflict resolution, with wide implications.

The Consortium grew out of an informal network. It retains its informal and flexible character, and this is the source of its strength. Individual NGOs have their own priorities, objectives, and programmes, reflecting their donors' interests, which they pursue in normal times. But in a crisis they come together to work in a co-ordinated way. This brings several advantages, including the benefits of a larger-scale operation and the ability to lobby for substantial funding because of their collective size and extensive contacts. Advantages also include the potential to draw on a wide range of partners in government, overseas governments, international agencies, and NGOs; and the Consortium's neutral position, derived from its diverse ethnic, religious, and geographic constituency. The 1996–7 food crisis in the Upper East Region again saw the Consortium activated to respond in a co-ordinated way, drawing on capacities built up during the Consortium's response to communal conflict. Unfortunately, funding constraints curtailed activities in this instance.

The peace process involved substantial co-operation with another southern NGO, the NPI. This is an excellent example of the value to be derived from South–South linking. The form taken by peace facilitation was holistic (ideologically 'African', according to the Kenyan NGO), and this proved highly appropriate for the context of northern Ghana. Not only did NPI's work lead to peace, it also built the capacities of NGOs and civil society to deal with future tension in this region, through providing tools for analysis and facilitation.

The creation and development of a strong, new civil-society organisation, NORYDA, is a significant positive outcome of the peace process. Working for sustainable peace with NGO financial and capacity-building support, it has already proved its effectiveness in the resolution of several outbreaks of conflict. This ability is based on the confidence and co-operation that NORYDA has earned among all stakeholders in civil society, because it is a creation of civil society. NORYDA has the plans and the potential to work and lobby for the equitable development of the Region for all.

8 Recommendations

For the Consortium

Consortium organisation and direction

Retain the informal and flexible character of the Consortium.

Build on the capacity of the Consortium by:

- Devising emergency-preparedness plans, including a division of roles and responsibilities. Formulating pro-active and preventative action plans.
- Incorporating more gender planning and analysis. This should apply to plans for crisis response, development, lobbying, and other plans, and include gender mapping within NGOs and the Consortium.
- Improving internal communications and overcoming the minor but significant difficulties of NGO co-ordination highlighted by the Consortium itself. Improving communication and co-operation between international and local NGOs. Promoting collaboration in analysis and planning between service-oriented and lobbying-oriented NGOs.
- Improve linkages with international donors (such as the UK Department for International Development) in order to appraise them of current issues.

- Improve linkages with local and national government, and particularly the REGSEC, to improve collaboration in terms of information-sharing and for conflict issues that may arise.

Consortium activities

Continue:

- To support the capacity-building of NORYDA to ensure the sustainability of the peace process. Support should also enable NORYDA to become truly representative of all ethnic groups in the Region.

Put in place:

- A training plan in peace facilitation with NGOs, government officials, and local leaders.
- Information-gathering for crisis early warning, given the highly uncertain and data-sparse context. Design a mechanism for communicating this information to NGOs in the south of Ghana, the government, the REGSEC, and donors, to ensure swift responses.

Table 7: NGO capacity-building needs

Skills	Requirements	Programme
Administrative capacity	Analysis of donor contacts	Emergency preparedness
Co-ordination among pluriform organisations	Common development planning	Rehabilitation planning and ongoing development programmes
Pro-active policy and advocacy design	Discussion of NGO roles	Continuing support to peace campaign in collaboration with local government
Building and monitoring capacity in local leadership	Constant redefinition of responsibilities between NGO and local leadership	NORYDA support
Gender-conscious analysis and planning	Higher priority	Co-ordination among international and local NGOs

Individual NGOs

- Continue to incorporate peace and reconciliation objectives in development work. Plan and monitor projects according to conflict-sensitivity indicators, to prevent bias that may heighten ethnic tensions.
- Improve development planning with local, regional, and national government.
- Share longer-term planning with other NGOs where appropriate, to prevent bias that may increase ethnic tensions.

Many NGOs require capacity-building in order to achieve these objectives. NGOs' needs in respect of capacity-building are summarised in Table 7.

For local government

Retain:
- Peace-promotion activities within local areas through schools, the NCCE, liaison with traditional authorities, and other appropriate channels.

Improve:
- The distribution of resources to ensure equity and to ensure that fairness is seen to be achieved, to prevent conflict over resources.
- The recognition of the value of NGO work and the NGO role in civil society.
- Communication and collaboration with NGOs in development planning through regular meetings at District level as well as Regional level. Bid to donors for funding for joint projects. Ensure that NGOs are accountable. Devise best-practice guidelines for all government departments, in collaboration with NGOs, to regulate human and material resource-management.
- Information-sharing with NGOs to promote communications with the grassroots and to avoid duplication of effort. Promote supportive networking agreements between government departments and NGOs.

For traditional authority and civil-society leaders

Build on:
- Reconciliation work at the grassroots level for a sustainable peace.
- The Kumasi Peace Accord. Agreements on creation of paramountcies should be adhered to. The Gonja–Nawuri dispute should be resolved at the earliest opportunity.

- Collaboration with local government in reconciliation and the development of political representation for all groups.
- Maintain support for NORYDA. Support its efforts to stand alone and to become a representative organisation of all ethnic groups in the Region. Increase its capacity to defuse conflicts. Support its development initiatives.

Also:
- The National and Regional Houses of Chiefs should work to improve representation of all ethnic groups by actively welcoming and co-operating with the new paramounts. Within a representative Northern House, a dialogue should be held on land issues as soon as possible, in consultation with other representatives of civil society, including NORYDA and the Consortium, and with relevant Ministry representatives. The House should also work on other conflict-related chieftaincy issues at the earliest opportunity.

For central government

Continue the successful (scaled-down) peace-keeping efforts for as long as necessary.

To address the root causes of the conflict:
- Design policy in order to support the equitable development of the Northern Region through local government and NGOs to end intra-regional and inter-regional disparities. Improve the distribution of resources so that it is fair and *seen* to be fair. Ensure that development and services are targeted to disadvantaged areas and ethnic groups. Attention should be paid to all aspects of development, but particularly to agriculture and education, including the provision of vocational training for young people.
- Facilitate participation in the democratic political process of the currently under-represented ethnic groups.
- Implement tighter arms-control policies.
- Recommend and promote government and NGO co-ordination and collaboration over peace initiatives and other activities at all levels. Recognise and support the Consortium-brokered peace agreement and end duplication/conflict of effort in this area.
- Recognise and support NORYDA's work.
- Act to defuse religion-based tensions. Ensure that NGOs are accountable in this context.

For donors

- Lobby for and support the equitable development of the Northern Region through local government and NGOs, to end intra-regional and inter-regional disparities.
- Support the Consortium's future activities, because this grouping has proved its advantages in terms of size, flexibility, and neutrality of status, particularly for crisis work.

- Research and recognise the problems inherent in channelling aid in terms of the potential for conflict and the effects of supporting NGO initiatives over government activities. Devise strategies to mitigate these outcomes.
- Recognise and support NORYDA as an organisation representative of all ethnic groups, to ensure the sustainability of the peace process. Assist NORYDA's institutional capacity-building and programme delivery.

Appendix 1: Example of workshop objectives, agenda, and rules (Kumasi II, 26–29 June 1995)[101]

Objectives

- To look at the conflict in the Northern Region and acquire an understanding of the damage done by the conflict.
- To understand what the conflict is about and assess its future direction.
- To analyse what needs to be done to respond to the conflict at various levels.
- To identify what we as participants should do, and what roles should be played by partners (NGO consortium, NPI).
- To agree on the next steps.

Agenda for the meeting

- Larger context: conflict in Africa; ethnicity.
- Conflict in the Northern Region of Ghana: assessing the damage.
- What is the conflict about? Exacerbating factors.
- What needs to be done?
- Difficulties and obstacles.
- Ways forward and next steps.
- Evaluation.
- Closing.

Ground rules

- Each person should have adequate time to express his views and perspective.
- Being sensitive to give others a chance and time to express their views also.
- Listening with respect, even if we do not agree. Avoid derogatory remarks.
- This meeting is *not a negotiation meeting*. The aim is to *understand* and not to debate.
- Everyone is acting in his individual capacity and not in the name of an organisation.
- Punctuality.

Appendix 2: peace achievements in detail (Kumasi I and II)[102]

Konkomba areas

- The Konkomba Youth Association (KOYA), the Nanumba Youth Association (NAYA), and the Bimbilla District Chief Executive collaborated to resolve the situation in Binchara-taanga. Konkombas had occupied Nanumba homes in some villages. It was agreed that after harvest they would leave those homes for the Nanumbas.
- KOYA has negotiated with the Dagomba Youth Association (DAYA) to return stolen cattle to their owners.
- A misunderstanding between Konkombas and Nanumbas at Nasu Village was resolved.
- KOYA organised a peace forum involving the chiefs and people of Saboba, Wapuli, and Kpalba to educate them on the values of peace.

Dagomba areas

- The PAC and DAYA helped to return a tractor and other personal belongings stolen from a Konkomba man.
- DAYA stopped the stealing and snatching of bicycles between Konkombas and Dagombas at Kulikpunduli Village, and cycles taken have been returned to their rightful owners.
- DAYA has made it possible for Konkombas to move freely to and from Yendi market to buy and sell, and for Konkomba Assemblymen to attend District Assembly meetings in Yendi.

Konkomba areas

- After the Kumasi workshops, NAYA held public meetings with Unit Committee members and the residents of Bimbilla, Wulensi, Nakpayili, and Pusuga to educate people on peace. This has also facilitated the free movement of people and goods. Konkombas now pass freely through these towns.
- NAYA have solved disputed cases of compensation involving cattle between Nanumbas and Konkombas.
- A dispute over the ownership of a bicycle was resolved, and a Konkomba was declared the rightful owner.
- There has been an agreement between NAYA and KOYA that the land and houses trespassed on by Konkombas will be returned to Nanumbas immediately after the crop harvest.

Generally there is now free movement of goods and people between Dagomba, Nanumba, and Konkomba settlements. Some of the disputes that could have resulted in open conflict are now resolved amicably among the factions.

Gonja–Nawuri–Nchumuru areas

While there are small efforts at peace building in the Gonja lands, attempts have been intensified to hold meetings with Gonja youths, chiefs, and people for peace education to ensure free movement of Konkombas and Gonjas in these areas.

After the third meeting of the PAC in Bimbilla on 26 August, the PAC and the PRWG visited the Nanumba paramount in Bimbilla and continued to Yendi to visit the Dagomba and Konkomba representatives. They were warmly received. In Saboba, a visit was made to the chief. Again, discussions were cordial and productive.

Appendix 3: Workshop evaluation statements (Kumasi II)[103]

Some samples of responses to this evaluation:

In these meetings, many of us saw our mistakes. Some of us would not even greet each other. Now after two years we are all smiles.

We learned the need for self-criticism in conflict situations.

I appreciated the possibility of interacting with various adversaries. The mature manner in which the meeting was conducted to allow various groups to express their feelings and experiences was most appreciated.

I learned that dialogue to solve the ethnic conflict in the north is possible ... The content of the meeting was very well planned to really bring out everything from the participants.

... all participants are very clear about the way to achieve lasting peace in the Northern Region.

I appreciate most the fact that all the main warring factions were able to come together to talk peace in earnest. We learned to respect one another.

From their statement at the beginning, there were people from all ethnic groups who were hard-liners when they first arrived. They now seem to feel and think differently. This means that this meeting has touched base with most people.

Security lies in ensuring the security of our enemy. In this way we put our enemy at ease. 'Strengthen your enemy.'

Appendix 4: Examples of grievances, losses, causes of the conflict, and action required, as expressed by workshop participants (Kumasi III)

Grievances of participants

Dagomba group

Damages/loss
- Great loss of human lives
- Displacement
- Deprivation and dependency
- Destruction of educational, social, and economic infrastructure
- Dislocation of social life
- Loss of trust, confidence and security
- Breeding of culture of violence
- Trauma

Causes of conflict
- Confusion over customary land rights
- Wilful refusal to acknowledge chiefs' titles and allegiance owed
- Disregard of chieftaincy laws relating to chieftaincy in Dagbon
- Disregard of judicial role of chiefs
- Attacks against Islam
- Discriminatory practices of some Christian NGOs
- Misinformation
- Unguarded statements by high-ranking government officials
- 'Konkombas are prone to fighting.'

Gonja group

Damages/loss
- Loss of life and property
- Strained relations with 'our brothers the Nawuris and Nchumurus'
- Loss of goodwill from outside, which has retarded development
- Break in traditional ties between Gonjas, Nawuris, Nchumurus
- Loss of mutual trust between Gonjas, Nawuris, Nchumurus

Causes of conflict
- Agitation for land by Nawuris and Nchumurus from Gonjas
- 'We cannot explain why there is conflict between us and Konkombas.'

Konkomba group

Damages/loss
- Broken marriages and friendships
- Loss of property, lives, educational and health facilities, drain on manpower, loss of marketing facilities
- Displaced people in their own country
- Politically isolated at District and national levels
- Cultural values broken down and undermined
- Destruction of places of worship i.e. churches/mosques
- Lack of trust among different religious faiths

Causes of conflict
- Denial of the right of the ruled to elect their leaders
- Imposition of leaders who are not popular with the governed
- Tendency of one tribe to feel superior to another
- Lack of respect for other people's cultural values
- Dominance of the minority over majority: of 16 ethnic groups, four rule
- Denial of the right to self-governance
- Use of derogatory term 'alien' for Konkombas
- Rumour

Nanumba group

Damages/loss
- Social
  - Loss of interaction between the two tribes
  - About 80 per cent of the population of war-torn areas became displaced
  - Increased migration from rural to urban areas
  - 56 villages were destroyed
  - Insecurity
  - People cannot farm and feed themselves
  - 34 schools and three health posts destroyed
  - Wulensi Senior Secondary School textbooks and electrical cables looted
  - Most schools not functioning in the district

- Economic
  - Most farms destroyed
  - 80 per cent of cattle herds stolen
  - Grinding mills, vehicles, bicycles and personal belongings lost
  - Property, including cash, lost
  - Economic interaction between the two tribes ceased

- Political
  - No District Assembly elections have been held
  - Lack of mutual trust between the two tribes

- Cultural
  - Eight Chiefs were killed, and their funerals have not been performed
  - Customary regalia and monuments destroyed
  - Traditional celebrations not fully observed

- Spiritual
  - Houses of worship destroyed

Causes of conflict
- Misinformation
- Enskinment of self-styled chiefs
- Settling without permission
- Main cause of the conflict in Nanun is the intention to seize Nanun lands by force of arms

Nawuri group

Damages/loss

- Social
  - Loss of lives, especially women's and children's
  - Displacement
  - Collapse of social structures e.g. communications
  - Education at a standstill
  - Fear and distrust

- Economic
  - Destruction of houses and property
  - Farming activities and trade halted
  - Loss of jobs, workers displaced

- Political
  - Breakdown of government administration e.g. District and Regional
  - Development projects halted

- Cultural
  - An aggressive future generation produced

- Spiritual
  - Bitterness left in the minds of people
  - Drift from the fear of God

Causes of conflict
- Political
  - Natural boundaries
  - Colonial administration policies

- Social
  - Post-independence disregard of Nawuri status
  - Imposition of chiefs from non-indigenous ethnic groups in the northern social system

- Religion
  - Suspicious agenda of certain religious organisations

- Culture
  - Distinct practices

- Economic
  - Destructive weapons (sophisticated warfare)

Nchumuru group

Damages/loss

- Economic
  - Loss of human life and property
  - Loss of farms and products
  - Disruption of economic activities
  - Destruction of commercial activities
  - Destruction of communication/trade routes
  - General economic stagnation

- Social
  - Disintegration of families
  - Dislocation of society
  - Migration and immigration
  - Insecurity and fear
  - Destruction of educational infrastructure and logistics
  - Exodus of educational and health/medical personnel

- Political
  - Non-participation in political decision-making e.g. District and Regional levels

- Cultural
  - Destruction of places of worship and activities of Christian bodies
  - At the psychological level: destruction of human values and social ethics

Causes of conflict

- Historical
  - Pre-colonial history
  - Colonial era under Germans and British
  - Indirect rule

- Social
  - Fragmentation of Region and Districts
  - Cultural assimilation
  - Lack of development and education

- Cultural
  - Representation of tribes at Regional House of Chiefs
  - Lack of recognition of our chiefs
  - Lack of involvement in decision-making at the District and Regional levels
  - Lack of cultural identity

- Political
  - Lack of representation and involvement in decision-making
  - Lack of political will on the part of government

Actions required or recommended

Dagomba

National level
- The NGO Consortium and NPI in contact with the Youth Associations should establish a national workshop, involving all the Executive members of the Youth Associations.
- Government should draw up a comprehensive programme for rehabilitation and reconstruction to repair medical, educational, and social infrastructure destroyed in the affected areas.
- There is a need to expand and strengthen the PPNT by including representatives from the various ethnic groups.

Regional level
- A Regional Peace Consultative committee should be formed with representatives from all the affected ethnic groups.
- For quick restoration of peaceful atmosphere, conciliatory gestures should be carried out:
  - by Konkombas, e.g. render sincere apology
  - by Dagomba Ya-Na to instruct all Dagombas to allow Konkombas access to all parts of Dagbon.

- There is a need to encourage interaction between Dagomba and Konkomba to promote peace and joint co-operative voluntary ventures.

Local level
- NGOs should embark on projects in areas where Dagombas and Konkombas live together.
- Mamprusis and Bimobas should be drawn into the peace efforts.

Gonja

National level
- National House of Chiefs should be involved.
- Findings of the National House of Chiefs should be sent to Government for discussion.

Regional level
- Regional House of Chiefs should be involved.
- Findings of Regional House of Chiefs should be passed to Regional Security Council.
- All Youth Associations should be involved.

Local level
- The Traditional Councils should be involved.
- District Security Councils should be involved.
- Opinion leaders should be involved.

Konkomba

National level
- PPNT needs to recognise and endorse the efforts of the NGO consortium/NPI i.e. Government recognition.
- Participants of workshop should write a letter of recommendation to the PPNT to that effect, with copies to religious bodies, National House of Chiefs, and Speaker of Parliament.

Regional level
- There should be a meeting of all Youth Leaders of all ethnic groups in the North with Consortium of NGOs.
- We recognise the effort being made to increase paramountcies in the Northern Region. However we wish to appeal to the Regional House of Chiefs to consider those ethnic groups with no representation in the House to facilitate peace and development.
- A working group should be formed, representing all ethnic groups in the region.

Local level
- Meet chiefs, opinion leaders, and youth leaders in Saboba and other Districts in the conflict area to educate people on the outcome of this workshop.

- There is a need for transport of workshop participants to other Districts of the conflict area.
- Workshop participants should give lectures to students of second-cycle institutions and churches and mosques.
- District Chief Executive should reflect the ethnicity of the District.

Nanumba

National level
- Adequate security should be provided to enable everyone to move about safely and freely.
- Halt the flow of arms and ammunition into the Region.
- Law and order should be strictly enforced.
- Security personnel should exhibit a high sense of discipline, honesty, and fairness.
- Those in authority should avoid inflammatory statements.
- Government should direct PPNT to offer maximum co-operation to the NGO Consortium/NPI.

Regional level
- Regional administration should encourage the creation of more paramountcies for other tribes.
- The Regional Minister should pay regular visits to the conflict areas.
- The Northern Youth Association should be reactivated.
- The NGO Consortium should hold a Regional Peace Seminar with the Regional House of Chiefs and all parties involved in the conflict.

Local level
- Extensive education on peace.
- Resettlement of displaced people.
- Rapid repairs to damaged education and health facilities.
- The paramount chief should have the prerogative to appoint chiefs.
- Committees of reconciliation must be established at local level.

Nawuri

National level
- Implementation of the findings of Committees of Enquiry.
- Enforcement of law and order.
- Information should be promptly investigated.

- Education on effects of conflicts e.g. radio programmes.
- Northern MPs should be part of the peace process.
- Rehabilitation.

Regional level
- Representation at the Regional House of Chiefs.
- Representation on the Regional Co-ordinating committee.
- Openness and fairness.

Local level
- All chiefs and opinion leaders should be involved in the peace process.
- More concerned Gonjas (from Kpembe) should be involved.
- Working groups should be assisted (funded) to explain the peace process at grassroots level.
- Involve other actors: women's groups, Muslim Council, Christian Council, and Catholic Secretariat, as well as the PPNT.

Nchumurus

National level
- Expansion of the National House of Chiefs.
- National leaders should be guarded in their pronouncements.
- More serious and objective attention should be given to rumours of conflict.
- Security in Northern Region should be strengthened.
- Membership of the Regional Security Council should be reviewed.

Regional level
- Regional House of Chiefs should be expanded to reflect ethnicity of the Region so as to create a forum for dialogue.
- Regional Security Committee should be objective and serious in handling ethnic problems in the region.
- More police posts/stations should be opened in conflict areas.
- Regional youth associations should be revived and used as agents for peace and interaction.
- Political leaders should be objective, open-minded, and fair in the administration of the Region.
- We should respect each other's religious views.

Local level

- Involvement of opinion leaders and stakeholders in the process of reconciliation.
- Meeting with various youth organisations and chiefs to spread the peace message.
- Opening channels of communication between groups in conflict.

- Recognition of the identity and views of other ethnic groups.
- Involvement of various ethnic groups in decision-making by traditional, chiefs, NGOs, government, Houses of Chiefs, youth movements, Information Services Department, and religious groups.

Appendix 5: Text of Kumasi Peace Accord

KUMASI ACCORD ON PEACE AND RECONCILIATION BETWEEN THE VARIOUS ETHNIC GROUPS IN THE NORTHERN REGION OF GHANA

INTRODUCTION

Since November 1994 the inter-NGO Consortium and the Nairobi Peace Initiative (NPI) have been organising and facilitating a series of peace and reconciliation consultations and workshops among the warring ethnic groups in Northern Ghana.

Follow-up and Planning committees were formed from the different ethnic groups in the region to work the NPI and the Consortium. Between May 1995 and April 1996 five meetings and consultations were organised in Kumasi as well as numerous others in Bimbilla, Gushegu/Karaga, Saboba, Salaga, Yendi, and Zabzugu/Tatale aimed at creating consensus on the need for peace and reconciliation, building confidence among the warring ethnic communities, as well as searching for solutions to the outstanding issues of conflict underlying the wars.

At the fourth Kumasi meeting, 48 delegates from seven ethnic groups constituting chiefs, PPNT delegates, opinion and youth leaders were invited to work towards the search for durable resolution to the conflicts in the Northern Region of Ghana. The NPI facilitated a series of bilateral and multilateral negotiations aimed at identifying the issues clearly and finding solutions that are acceptable to all the parties involved. On February 29, 1996, the delegates severally and jointly agreed to a draft document which outlined the agreements reached on the contentious issues presented in the negotiations.

The draft agreement was then taken by the delegates to their respective communities for extensive consultation, discussion and feedback with all segments of their community. After four weeks, the delegates returned to Kumasi to report on the outcome of their consultation processes, to incorporate into the draft agreement the feed-back and amendments generated by the consultations, as well as, when necessary, to renegotiate the draft agreement. After these processes, on March 30th 1996, the delegates signed the following document which was called the Kumasi Accord on Peace and Reconciliation Between The Various Ethnic Groups In The Northern Region of Ghana.

PREAMBLE

WE, the Bassare, Dagomba, Gonja, Konkomba, Nanumba, Nawuri and Nchumuru delegations:

MEETING together at the Peace and Reconciliation Consultations held in Kumasi in February and March 1996;

HAVING heard, considered, discussed and debated the demands each group had against each other as adversaries during the Northern Region conflict;

BELIEVING that all ethnic communities have a crucial role to play in the building of peace;

DETERMINED to resolve all outstanding issues between us and to lay the foundation for a durable and stable peace for sustainable development;

CONVINCED that it is in the best interest of our respective people that we create an enabling atmosphere of peace that will foster social re-integration, mobility, economic cooperation and development as individuals and as groups;

ACCEPTING that our individual and group aspirations of development can only be achieved in an atmosphere of forgiveness, moderation, compromise, cooperation and the peaceful resolution of our differences;

NOW AGREE as follows:

AGREEMENTS BETWEEN THE DAGOMBAS, KONKOMBAS AND BASSARES

1 The present scheme of land tenure in Dagbon reflected in the customary laws, usages and practices is non-discriminatory and satisfies the aspirations of all citizens of Dagbon regardless of ethnic background. It is recognised that the Ya-Na holds the allodial title to all Dagbon lands and he holds same as a trustee in trust for all the citizens of Dagbon. The divisional chiefs whether they are Dagombas, Konkombas, Bassares etc are the caretakers of the land and all citizens through their respective divisions have a birth-right of equal and unimpeded access to the land in accordance with customary law. In this context the term "citizens" refers to all persons claiming and reputed to be indigenous persons and recognised as such. Currently Dagombas, Konkombas, Bassares, Anufos etc. are generally known as citizens.

2 We are appreciative of the Ya-Na's gesture to confer paramountcy on Dagomba, Konkomba, Bassare etc. chiefs and note with satisfaction that the conditions attached to the elevation to paramountcy are as applicable to Dagomba chiefs as they are to Konkomba and Bassare chiefs in the same situation.

3 We note with satisfaction that even before the conflict Konkomba, Bassare and Anufo chiefs had representation in the Dagbon Traditional Council. We also note that the participation of these chiefs in the Dagbon Traditional Council was interrupted when the conflict broke out. We agree that the said chiefs ought to resume their active participation in the work of the Traditional Council.

4 We declare and affirm our acceptance and observance of the rules, customs, practices and usages regarding the institution of chieftaincy in Dagbon and that without discrimination all chiefs in Dagbon, be they Dagombas, Konkombas, Bassares, Anufos, etc. are entitled to exercise all powers, jurisdiction and authority reserved for chiefs under customary law.

In particular we affirm that all chiefs in Dagbon, save and except as custom or the law may limit, are entitled to exercise all rights and powers in the following matters, namely:-
a. the creation and approval of new settlements in the area of jurisdiction
b. enskinments of lesser chiefs or headmen in the area of jurisdiction
c. the prerogative to adjudicate upon certain disputes in the area of jurisdiction
d. entitlement to jurisdictional allegiance from subjects in the area of jurisdiction.

5 We will respect and be sensitive to the respective religious subscribed to by our people and we shall do nothing that will directly or indirectly offend, impugn or ridicule each other's religion.

6 We decry the spiral of arms and ammunition build-up in the Northern Region and affirm our readiness and determination to stem their flow into the region.

7 We declare that we shall cooperate fully in bringing about and facilitating a complete reconciliation of our people in accordance with the tenets of our customs. We note in particular the restrictions on the movement of Konkombas and Bassares in Tamale and other areas in the Region and agree that we shall implement such appropriate measures as may be found efficacious to ease the problem.

8 As an assurance to our continued peaceful co-existence and collaborative relations we undertake to cease all provocative acts, utterance and particularly publications in the media that may inflame passions and lead to breaches of security in our areas.

9 We recognise and accept the value of confidence-building in our efforts to structure and entrench peace and we therefore agree that in all our dealings with each other we shall demonstrate absolute good faith, sincerity and commitment to peace.

AGREEMENTS BETWEEN THE KONKOMBAS AND NANUMBAS

1 Nanumbas, who are indigenous and sole owners of the land in Nanun, do recognise the Konkombas as an important non-Nanumba community and brothers in development who seek the well-being of the district and whose status, rights, duties and obligations are traditionally recognised and defined under Nanun customary law and usage.

2 Konkombas shall be allowed to freely choose their headmen to be blessed by the Bimbilla-Naa or his delegated divisional authority, provided this will not conflict with the interest of the Bimbilla-Naa and/or the Princes of Nanun.

3 Representation at administrative and political decision-making processes shall be by merit and following due process.

4 We declare that we shall cooperate fully in bringing about and facilitating a complete reconciliation of our people in accordance with the tenets and practices of our traditions. We note in particular the restriction on the movement of our peoples in Nanun and all the other areas in the Region and agree that we shall implement appropriate measures as may be found efficacious to ease the problem.

5 Land ownership is not in dispute with the Bimbilla-Naa as the paramount chief and allodial owner of all land in Nanun as accepted by the Konkombas.

6 Paramountcy is the preserve of eligible Nanumbas.

7 We shall accept regulations from the Nanumba Traditional Council with Konkomba representation, which, with the help of ecological experts, regulates land use, land tenure and settlement patterns for purposes of preservation of the ecology for future generations.

8 Customary pacification in respect of river gods, land gods and groves should only be performed by the recognised land and fetish priests or Tindanas of Nanun.

9 We agree to refrain from the practice of ethnicising individual criminal behaviour; that is, from blaming an entire ethnic group for the criminal conduct of an individual who is a member of that ethnic group.

10 For purposes of assuring security and the avoidance of recurrent inter-communal violence, the parties agree to create committees composed of Nanumbas and Konkombas whose tasks will consist of the following:
   a. identifying people in Nanun communities that foment or incite ethnic animosity and violence and ensure that appropriate legal actions are taken against such people in order to stop or deter their behaviour.
   b. Identifying particularly conflict-sensitive areas and travelling to those areas jointly (Konkombas and Nanumbas together) to educate people about peaceful co-existence and to resolve problems in the areas peacefully so that inter-communal violence does not erupt.

11 On the issue of the 365 self-styled chiefs and separatists, we the Konkomba delegation will undertake, with the assistance of the Nanumba delegation, to verify and ascertain the position of such chiefs and in consultation with our Nanumba counterparts seek a solution that will be satisfactory to both sides.

12 We decry the spiral of arms and ammunition build-up in the Northern Region and affirm our readiness and determination to stem their flow into the region.

AGREEMENTS BETWEEN THE GONJAS AND NCHUMURUS

1 The Nchumurus have appealed to the Gonjas not to frustrate Nanjuro-Wura's application for paramountcy. Gonjas have agreed to cooperate.

2 Gonjas have accepted in principle that the Nanjuro-Wura's status had been established as equivalent to a divisional chief. It was circumstances that made him opt out of the Gonja chieftaincy system.

3 Gonjas will allow the Nanjuro-Wura's application through Government, for paramountcy to go through at the National House of Chiefs.

4 The Gonjas also agree to support a subsequent creation of separate Nchumuru Traditional Council.

5 The Nchumurus will have representation on Northern Region House of Chiefs.

6 In order to facilitate these agreements, the following steps have been agreed upon by the two sides:
   a. The Gonja delegation will immediately brief the Yagbon-Wura and the Kpembe-Wura on Nchumura proposals and demands.
   b. The Tuluwe-Wura will liaise with the Mion-Lana (AA Ziblim) who has agreed to act as an intermediary between Nchumuru and Gonja.
   c. In consequence of item (b) above, the Mion-Lana and Tuluwe-Wura have scheduled to visit the Yagbon-Wura on the 15th of March to concretise the Gonja–Nchumuru peace process.
   d. The Mion-Lana will give a feedback, subsequent to which Nchumuru will propose a tentative date to meet with the Yagbon-Wura. The date should allow sufficient notice to enable the Yagbon-Wura to assemble his divisional chiefs.

61

7   A preliminary meeting between Gonja and Nchumuru at the highest Traditional Level should open the avenues for the formulation of Peace-Awareness groups/meetings/workshops at the community levels.

8   Both ethnic groups will commence organising their peoples for reintegration, resettlement and reconstruction.

9   The follow-up Committee will be invited to facilitate the plans/expectations above.

AGREEMENTS BETWEEN THE KONKOMBAS AND GONJAS

1   We commit ourselves to express respect to each other and refrain from activities that debase or insult each other's people, elders, customs and traditions.

2   Konkombas have no claim to Gonja land or to paramountcy in the same area. However, where there is a large Konkomba community, the Gonja paramount or divisional chief may confer a leadership title that he deems fit on any Konkomba who will serve under him.

3   We agree that when conflicts erupt or rumours about conflicts circulate, the chiefs and leaders from the Gonja and Konkomba communities will take initiatives to approach each other to investigate the matter and arrest the escalation through respectful discussions.

4   The Konkombas agree to undertake an independent investigation of the causes for the 1994 war between them and the Gonjas and share their findings so that both parties could learn from the mistakes that might have been committed by any side and put mechanisms in place to ensure that the same mistakes are not committed again.

5   In order to encourage free movement in the conflict areas as an element of reconciliation between Gonjas and Konkombas, we agree:
   a. That we shall ask our respective chiefs, headmen, elders, youth association leaders to ensure safe movement of members of the other ethnic group within their communities.
   b. That if anyone from another ethnic group is attacked we agree to hold the chief or leader accountable to apprehend the culprit or be held accountable themselves.
   c. That working groups made up of representatives of all ethnic groups in the area follow up at the community levels and educate citizens on the need for peaceful coexistence and free movement.
   d. A peace conference will be organised in Salaga before the commencement of the farming season involving all ethnic groups in the Salaga area.

AGREEMENTS BETWEEN THE BASSARES AND GONJAS

1   Both sides recognise that the investigation of the Buipe Bridge incident is an essential ingredient in the reconciliation process between Bassares and Gonjas.

2   The Gonjas agree to undertake an independent investigation into the matter and share the findings so that both parties could learn from the mistakes that might have been committed by any side and to put mechanisms in place to ensure that the same mistake is not committed again.

3   Bassares have no claim to Gonja land or to paramountcy in the same area. However, where there is a large Bassare community, the Gonja paramount or divisional chief may confer a leadership title that he deems fit on any Bassare who will serve under him.

AGREEMENTS BETWEEN THE NAWURIS AND GONJAS

1   The Nawuris and the Gonjas recognise that there are several outstanding issues of dispute between them that require peaceful resolution. The Kumasi meetings have helped both delegations to articulate and identify these issues.

2   The two delegations agree to continue the dialogue that has begun in Kumasi in order to create a conducive environment and understanding that would lead to the resolution of the outstanding issues.

3   To that effect, the Nawuris agree to intensify their confidence-building and peace-education activities to encourage peaceful ethnic co-existence in their respective communities with the assistance of the Peace Awareness Committee.

4   The Nawuris agree to assist, in whatever way possible, in resettling the Gonjas displaced from Kpandai due to the war between the two ethnic groups in 1991, back in the places from which they were displaced.

AGREEMENT ON REGIONAL ASSOCIATION

To underline our commitment to this Accord, and to enshrine the sense of unity that the Accord generates among us signatories and our peoples in the Northern Region of Ghana, as well as to give an institutional embodiment to the spirit of this Accord which can enhance the implementation of the Accord's provisions, we have hereby agreed to create a region-wide association that will be composed of representatives from all the ethnic communities which currently live in the Northern Region. The specific nature and functions of such an association shall be determined at a meeting of representatives of youth associations from all ethnic communities in Northern Ghana and this meeting shall be organised to take place immediately subsequent to the signing of this Accord.

IN FULL AGREEMENT with the above paragraphs, we the delegates from the seven ethnic communities in the Northern Region of Ghana have signed this Accord on this 30th day of March, 1996 in Kumasi, the capital of the Ashanti Region of Ghana.

(34 signatures follow)

Notes

1 EIU 1996–97:13, Austin 1996:553–60, Sarris and Shams 1991:8.
2 Glewwe and Twum-Baah 1991:47–9.
3 Nyakora 1994:2.
4 Sarris and Shams 1991.
5 Nyakora 1994:2.
6 UNDP 1997.
7 Goody 1968.
8 Promoting irrigated rice cultivation, soya, and maize crops, it mainly benefits ex-civil servants and non-farmers.
9 Funded by the Sasakawa Foundation, but channelled through MoFA extension services.
10 Groups which lay claim to having origins in this Region. There are many 'temporary' residents from groups outside the Region, such as civil servants and Fulani cattle-keepers.
11 Traditionally, they have not had chiefs or other forms of permanent leadership.
12 Pul 1994a:1.
13 The estimate for the Dagombas refers to 1981. Figures from Barker 1986:170 and Staniland 1985:32.
14 Ollennu and Woodman 1985.
15 This type of control is implied in the term *naam*, meaning 'chieftaincy'.
16 According to Skalnik 1983:23.
17 Recently there has been a rise in urban land sales, including a tenfold increase in the value of urban land over the past four years.
18 Goody 1979.
19 Norton, 1990:4.
20 Known as a 'gate' in the north.
21 i.e. the extent of their power over people rather than over territory; although, as suggested, territoriality is being increasingly applied as a concept. The term is from Drucker-Brown 1975.
22 Tait 1969, Staniland 1975.
23 There are no secular leaders. Political organisation is maintained through the structural opposition between lineage segments at different levels (from a small family unit to the clan) and cross-cutting ties of alliance (such as religious and marital). Traditional priests often play a

strong role in dispute settlement and leadership in acephalous societies.
24 Here, a particular leg of a large kill is given to the local chief.
25 See Figure 4.
26 NPI and Inter-NGO Consortium 1995b: 1.
27 See Figure 4.
28 For example, Saaka notes (1978:126), writing on the Gonja Districts, 'in the smaller villages (where most people live) the only legitimate political authority is the chief. It is thus not incongruous for the people to accept traditional authorities as intermediaries between them and modern government.'
29 Goody 1979.
30 The Mamprusi are an exception.
31 Sources: interviews, press statements, and workshop reports.
32 Skalnik 1983:20.
33 Drucker-Brown 1997.
34 November 1994.
35 Pul 1994a.
36 *Ibid.*
37 *Ibid*: 3.
38 GBC 1994.
39 GBC 1994.
40 MoFA 1995:6.
41 Regional Technical Committee 1994:9.
42 MoFA 1994:2.
43 Regional Technical Committee 1994:8.
44 Inter-NGO Consortium 1994a.
45 Inter-NGO Consortium 1994a.
46 The operation commander had undertaken a thorough analysis of the conflict, showing how the Konkombas had mobilised for war by moving entire Konkomba communities into attacking positions, drawing on women to provide logistics, whereas the cephalous communities had called on their warrior clans to fight. The Konkomba tactics made it difficult for cephalous groups to attack, because Konkombas hid in clusters in the bush. He concluded that cephalous groups were weakened in this context by the participation of the younger warrior clan members in education and urban life. They no longer wished to fight or travel to the

rural areas and did not feel strong obligations to do so. Many cephalous urban youths, filled with bravado, who did board trucks in Tamale to join the fight elsewhere, ran away when they saw the realities of conflict. Konkomba youths, on the other hand, tended to remain in rural areas, not having had so many educational opportunities, and were ready to fight.

47 Scarcity of food, poor health, crop destruction, reduced animal and poultry production, and continued animal theft were cited as the greatest problems in the report. Needs were assessed as agricultural inputs (seed, tractor service, reinstatement of credit and banking facilities, of disease and pest control and other services disrupted due to the exodus of civil servants).

48 MoFA 1994:1–12.

49 These include membership organisations, church-related professional NGOs, and NGOs with a small professional team.

50 Now Department for International Development (DFID).

51 MoFA 1995:7.

52 *Ibid.*

53 UNICEF 1995.

54 Bacho, Musah and Mahama 1996.

55 NPI and Inter-NGO Consortium 1995a:1.

56 Pul 1994a:3.

57 Capital of the Ashanti Region.

58 Assefa 1993.

59 *Ibid.*

60 The NPI believes that multipartyism in Africa has led to current strife.

61 Pugansoa 1996:3–4.

62 NPI and Inter-NGO Consortium 1995b:4.

63 NPI and Inter-NGO Consortium 1995a:2.

64 NPI and Inter-NGO Consortium June 1995:5.

65 NPI and Inter-NGO Consortium June 1995:9.

66 Jessiwuni 1995:4–5.

67 *Ibid.*

68 Inter-NGO Consortium 1995a: 9.

69 Pugansoa 1996:4.

70 NPI and Inter-NGO Consortium 1995b:6.

71 *Ibid*: 6–8.

72 Inter-NGO Consortium 1995:2.

73 Notably, the Bassares did not participate in the Kumasi series. They declined to do so because they were not directly involved in the 1994–5 conflict and did not want to be regarded as allies of any other group. However, they were signatories to the Kumasi Peace Accord.

74 NPI and Inter-NGO Consortium 1995a:1–2.

75 NPI and Inter-NGO Consortium 1995a.

76 *Ibid*: 14–5.

77 Further responses are listed in Appendix 3.

78 Consortium June 1995:7.

79 Consortium June 1995:7.

80 Pugansoa 1996:4.

81 Inter-NGO Consortium 1996b:1–2.

82 Detailed in Appendix 10.8.

83 NPI and Inter NGO consortium 1995a: 1.

84 BBC (1997).

85 Nyakora 1995:6.

86 Nyakora 1995:6.

87 Ethnic group adjacent to the main Konkomba area in the Saboba-Chereponi District (see Figure 2).

88 The Regional Co-ordinating Council is a Government body consisting of representatives of a number of government departments, including the Ministry of the Interior and the Military Task Force.

89 Nyakora 1995:7.

90 Bacho, Musah, and Mahama 1996:30.

91 Bacho, Musah, and Mahama 1996:37.

92 *Ibid.*

93 Pul 1994b: 2–4.

94 NPI and Inter-NGO Consortium 1995a:4.

95 *Ibid.*

96 Bacho, Musah and Mahama 1996:37.

97 Bacho, Musah and Mahama 1996:36.

98 These are said to have political links with the government and the opposition respectively.

99 The *Northern Monitor*, a Dagomba-dominated paper, even criticised the election of a Mamprusi head for NORYDA recently, on the grounds that Mamprusis 'swerved' the conflict, that is, that they did not come to the aid of the other cephalous groups!

100 Inaugurated September 1996.

101 NPI and Inter-NGO Consortium 1995a.

102 NPI and Inter-NGO Consortium 1995b:10–11.

103 NPI and Inter-NGO Consortium 1995a.

References

Published and broadcast material

Abbink, J. (1997) 'Staatsvorming in Afrika' (State formation in Africa), *Internationale Spectator*, 51(4): 204–8

Abudulai, M. S. (1986) 'Land tenure among the Dagomba of Northern Ghana: empirical evidence', *Cambridge Anthropology* 11(3):72–103

Amankwah, H. A. (1989) *The Legal Regime of Land Use in West Africa: Ghana and Nigeria*, Hobart, Tasmania: Pacific Law Press

Assefa, H. (1993) *Peace and Reconciliation as a Paradigm: A philosophy of peace and its implications on conflict, governance and economic growth in Africa*, Nairobi: Nairobi Peace Initiative

Austin, G. (1996) 'National poverty and the "Vampire State" in Ghana: a review article', *Journal of International Development* 8(4): 553–73

Barker, P. (1986) *Peoples, Languages and Religion in Northern Ghana*, Accra: Asempa

BBC (British Broadcasting Corporation) (1996) 'Balls to Africa', London: BBC

Buijtenhuis, R. and E. Rijnierse (1993) *Democratisation in Sub-Saharan Africa 1989–1992*, Leiden: Afrika-Studiecentrum

Cairns, E. (1997) *A Safer Future: Reducing the Human Cost of War*, Oxford: Oxfam

van Cranenburgh, O. (1997) 'Meerpartijenverkiezingen in Afrika' (Multi party elections in Africa), *Internationale Spectator* 51(4): 214–7

Drucker-Brown, S. (1975) *Ritual Aspects of the Mamprusi Kingship*, Leiden: Afrika-Studiecentrum

Drucker-Brown, S. (1995) 'Communal violence in Northern Ghana: unaccepted warfare' in R. A. Hinde and H. E. Watson (eds) *War: a Cruel Necessity?: the Bases of Institutionalised Violence*, London: Tauris

Economist Intelligence Unit (1996) *Ghana Country Profile: 1996–7*, London: EIU

Economist Intelligence Unit 1997) *Ghana Country Report: First Quarter 1997*, London: EIU

Ellis, S. (1997) 'Nieuwe machtspatronen in Afrika' (New Patterns of Governance in Africa), *Internationale Spectator* 51(4): 201–3

Gary, I. (1996) 'Confrontation, co-operation or co-optation: NGOs and the Ghanaian state during structural adjustment', *Review of African Political Economy*, 68(2–3): 149–68.

Gayi, S. K. (1995) 'Adjusting to the social costs of adjustment in Ghana: problems and prospects', *The European Journal of Development Research*, 7(1): 77–100

GBC (Ghana Broadcasting Corporation) (1994) 'Special Programme: Ethnic Conflict in the Northern Region', Accra: GBC

Glewwe, P. and K. A. Twum-Baah (1991) 'The Distribution of Welfare in Ghana, 1987–8', *LSMS Working Paper No. 75*, Washington DC: World Bank

Goody, J. R. (1968) 'Restricted literacy in Northern Ghana' in J. R. Goody (ed.), *Literacy in Traditional Societies*, Cambridge: Cambridge University Press

Goody, J.R. (1979) 'Rice-burning and the Green Revolution in Northern Ghana', *The Journal of Development Studies* 16(2):136–55

Grove, D. (1963) 'Population patterns', in *Planning Research Studies* 1, Kumasi: UST

Hailu, Z. (1990) *The Adoption of Modern Farm Practices in African Agriculture*, Weikersheim, Germany: Verlag Josef Margraf

Holtkamp, T. (1993) *Dezentralisierung und Partizipation in Ghana*, Saarbrucken, Germany: Verlag Breitenbach

Ladouceur, P. (1979) *Chiefs and Politicians: The Politics of Regionalism in Northern Ghana*, London: Longman

Lentz, C. (1995) 'Unity for development, Youth Associations in North-Western Ghana', *Africa*, 65 (3): 395–429

Nukunya, G. K. (1992) *Tradition and Change in Ghana: An Introduction to Sociology*, Accra: Ghana Universities Press

Ollennu, N.A. and G.R. Woodman (eds) (1985) *Ollennu's Principles of Customary Land Law in Ghana* (2nd ed.), Birmingham: CAL Press

Republic of Ghana, National Commission on Civic Education (1992) 'The Constitution Abridged' Accra: NCCE

Runge-Metzger, A., and L. Diehl (1993) *Farm Household Systems in Northern Ghana*, Weikersheim, Germany: Verlag Josef Margraf

Saaka, Y. (1978) *Local Government and Political Change in Northern Ghana*, Washington DC: University Press of America

Sarris, A. and H. Shams (1991) *Ghana Under Structural Adjustment: The Impact on Agriculture and the Rural Poor*, New York: New York University Press/IFAD

Shepherd, A. (1981) 'Agrarian change in Northern Ghana: public investment, capitalist farming and famine' in J. Heyer, P. Roberts and G. Williams (eds), *Rural Development in Tropical Africa*, London: Macmillan

Skalnik, P. (1983) 'Questioning the concept of the state in indigenous Africa', *Social Dynamics* 9(2): 11–28

Staniland, M. (1975) *The Lions of Dagbon: Political Change in Northern Ghana*, Cambridge: Cambridge University Press

Tait, D. (1961) *The Konkomba of Northern Ghana*, Oxford: Oxford University Press

UNDP (1997) *Human Development Report 1997*, New York: UNDP

Unpublished material

Bacho F. Z. I., E.K. Musah and A. Mahama (1996) 'Report on the Assessment of Rehabilitation Needs of Victims in the Conflict Area of the Northern Region', Tamale: Inter-NGO Consortium

Council of Churches Ghana (1995a) Annual Reports of the Committee on Co-operation

Council of Churches Ghana (1995b) 'Report of One-day Seminar on "Voices of women" from the Churches', Tamale: Christian Council of Ghana, November 1995

Council of Churches Ghana (1996) 'Programmes of Relief, Rehabilitation of Local Council of Churches', July–December 1996

Council of Churches Ghana (1996) 'The Role of Churches in the Democratic Process in Northern Ghana', Seminar Proposal, Tamale: Local Council of Churches, the Archdiocese and the Association of Church Development Projects

Dagomba Traditional Council (1995) 'On Petition of Saboba-na for Paramountcy and Traditional Council', Yendi

Drucker-Brown, S. (1997) 'Warfare in Northern Ghana', seminar held at University College London, 21 February 1997

Gubkatimali, Peronudas and Amasachina (1994) 'Assessment of Conflict Areas in Northern Region, Ghana', Tamale, May 1994

Inter-NGO Consortium (1994) 'Assessment of Situation in Conflict Areas of Ghana's Northern Region'

Inter-NGO Consortium (1995a) 'Proposal for a Second Workshop on Rehabilitation and Development Supported by the Inter-NGO Consortium', Accra: Inter-NGO Consortium, 22 June 1995

Inter-NGO Consortium (1995b) 'Inter-NGO Consortium and the Nairobi Peace Initiative's Six Months Peace and Reconciliation Activity Proposal', Accra and Tamale: Inter-NGO Consortium, September 1995

Inter-NGO Consortium (1996a) 'Kumasi Accord on Peace and Reconciliation Between the Various Ethnic Groups in the Northern Region of Ghana', Kumasi, May 1996

Inter-NGO Consortium (1996b) 'Report on the Northern Youth and Development Association Meeting held in Kumasi on October 11–13, 1996 to Ratify the Constitution of NORYDA as part of the Peace and Reconciliation Programme supported by the NGO Consortium', Tamale: Inter-NGO Consortium

Jesiwuni, I. (1995) 'The Issue of Conflicts in Africa: Focus on Conflicts in Northern Region of Ghana', Tamale: Inter-NGO Consortium processed

MoFA (Ministry of Food and Agriculture) (1994) 'Report on Tour of the Conflict Area of the Northern Region by the Minister for Food and Agriculture', 20–25 June 1994

Nairobi Peace Initiative and Inter-NGO Consortium (1995a) 'Second Workshop on Peace, Reconciliation and Development in the Northern Region of Ghana 26–9 June 1995', Tamale: Inter-NGO Consortium processed

Nairobi Peace Initiative and Inter-NGO Consortium (1995b) 'Search for Peace in the Northern Region of Ghana. Update report and six months' programme proposal', June Tamale: Inter-NGO Consortium

Norton, A. (1990) 'Report on a Mission of Pre-identification for ACORD, Northern Ghana', University College of Swansea: Centre for Development Studies

Nyakora, G. (1994) 'Case study: Peace and Reconciliation Workshop 18th–23rd July 1994, Jinja Uganda. Action Aid Ghana, Conflict in the Northern Region Republic of Ghana'

Nyakora, G. (1995) 'Case study: Understanding Peace and Conflict Management'

Oxfam GB (1994) 'Update on Northern Region Rehabilitation Programme', July 1994, Tamale: Oxfam GB

Pugansoa, B. (1996) 'The Northern Region of Ghana's Conflict of 1994: Some Responses, Problems and Opportunities', Tamale: Oxfam GB

Pul, H.A.S. (1994a) 'Agenda for Peace: A Position Paper on the Role of the Inter-NGO Consortium on the Northern Region's Conflict Resolution Process', Tamale: CRS processed

Pul, H.A.S. (1994b) ' Notes from the Meetings with the NPI Team on the Role of NGOs in Northern Conflict Resolution', Tamale: CRS Memorandum

Regional Technical Committee (1994) 'A Programme for the Resettlement of Displaced Persons from the Northern Region Ethnic Conflict', May 1994, Tamale: Regional Technical Committee

UNICEF (1995) 'Assessment of the Emergency Preparedness and response of the Inter-NGO Consortium', Accra: UNICEF

Also various minutes, memoranda, and facsimile communications.

Ada van der Linde was formerly Oxfam's Representative in Chad. She works as a training and education co-ordinator for the European Centre for Conflict Prevention. Rachel Naylor is a Research Officer with The Rural Development Council of Northern Ireland, working on a participatory development project jointly with Queen's University, Belfast.

Intense fighting in the Northern Region of Ghana in 1994 and 1995 led to the loss of 15,000 lives and the displacement of 200,000 people. A formal peace treaty, negotiated by the government, ended the fighting but did not address the underlying causes of the conflict, which were a complex mix of economic, political, and ethnic factors.

An informal consortium of NGOs, initially involved in delivering humanitarian aid, set up a parallel peace process, seeking to build up trust through a series of peace-education workshops and the creation of a multi-ethnic Youth and Development Association. The success of the process was symbolised by the signing of the Kumasi Peace Accord in 1996.

This report, commissioned by the Northern Ghana Inter-NGO Consortium, demonstrates how a network of NGOs, sharing skills and building up local capacities, can play an invaluable role in promoting a sustainable peace after conflict.

ISBN 0-85598-423-6 NBZI

9 780855 984236 >

Oxfam